The Prayer Manifesto for the Globally Conscious

The Prayer Manifesto for the Globally Conscious

How to Develop a Heart to Pray for Others

Lischa T. Brooks

iUniverse, Inc.
Bloomington

The Prayer Manifesto for the Globally Conscious
How to Develop a Heart to Pray for Others

iUniverse books may be ordered through booksellers or by contacting:

iUniverse
1663 Liberty Drive
Bloomington, IN 47403
www.iuniverse.com
1-800-Authors (1-800-288-4677)

ISBN: 978-1-4759-6504-9 (sc)
ISBN: 978-1-4759-6505-6 (e)
ISBN: 978-1-4759-6506-3 (hc)

Library of Congress Control Number: 2012922747

Printed in the United States of America

iUniverse rev. date: 12/21/2012

Contents

Acknowledgments

Everything I am, everything I have, everything that is good and perfect in my life comes from God. Every mountain, every roadblock, every situation that tried to knock me out of this race is nothing when compared to the love and faithfulness of God. Every day, every minute, every second of my life is given to me because of God's purposes for my life. Thank you, Father, for who you are and continue to be to me.

I would like to acknowledge my best friend, companion, and husband of fifteen years, Harold Brandon Brooks. He is the love of my life and has been my most ardent supporter since high school. He is the father of our two wonderful boys, known as the Brooks Brothers, Aldon Marcell and Andrew Miles. I thank God for my sons and for my goddaughter, Tanzye Marie Hill. Collectively, my brood is known as the M&Ms (Marie, Marcell, and Miles). They are like chocolate to my sweet tooth, and I cannot get enough of them!

My mother, Alberdeen "De" Clayborn, has been a constant supporter and mentor. She instilled in me from a young age that I should always do my best in everything I do and to "speak distinctively so people can understand you." She is a fighter and the most beautiful woman I know. My other parents, Bettye and Harold Brooks, have always been a blessing to our family, and I love them dearly. I would also like to acknowledge my brother, Marion, who has the most compassionate and loving spirit.

I thank God for the Clayborn sisters, Rosella, Dorothy Jean, Johnnie, and Mary Virginia—much of who I am today is because of who they were to me. They are women of God who are faithful members of their church communities and families. The memory of my grandmother Ozell Clayborn is a constant reminder of the Proverbs 31 woman, and I know I will see her again one day.

My pastors, John and Leslie Siebeling, have such a heart for God's people, and I am indebted to them and their staff for their obedience to start the Second Mile leadership program at my church. My participation in this leadership program was the catalyst for my finishing this book. The experience of finishing Second Mile opened a door for me in my spiritual walk, and I love my Life Church family for it. I would also like to thank Travis and Carol Moody for reading my manuscript and being supportive throughout this process.

Introduction

Job, once considered a wealthy and prosperous man, lost all his camels, sheep, donkeys, oxen, and, most importantly, his children. His health was failing him as his body was covered in painful sores. Job's wife added to his grief by telling him to curse God and die. The only thing worse that could have happened to Job was death. Job's friends blamed him for the current state of events and were not very good friends to him at all. How could Job's life get any worse? In the face of all Job was experiencing, God instructed him to pray for his friends (Job 42:8). Job had lost everything that was precious to him. He was beginning to question everything.

Have you ever been in a state of mind where you wondered whether God was aware of what you were experiencing or if your suffering would ever end? When faced with challenges, is your initial reaction to pray for others? In the midst of his suffering, however, Job was instructed by God to pray for the friends that should have comforted and encouraged him. Instead, they lied about God and blamed Job for his own misfortunes. After he prayed, something miraculous happened. Everything Job lost was restored, and he received even greater blessings. Job's decision to obey God and pray for someone else was the catalyst for his own restoration. Job prayed many times for himself and his situation, but it was not until he prayed for his friends that we see a change in his situation (Job 42:10).

James writes that when we pray with selfish motives, our prayers are hindered (James 4:3). James goes on to remind us that we are to pray for each other so we can be healed (James 5:16). According to the Amplified Bible, being healed refers to being healed and restored to a spiritual tone of mind and heart. Our own spiritual health and well-being, therefore, is directly related to our commitment to pray for one another. If you would not like your prayers to be hindered and you desire to have a healthy physical and spiritual life, you must commit to praying for one another. Let's make the commitment now!

In this book, I am looking at prayer from a different perspective. Most books about prayer focus only on the principles for getting personal prayers answered, or how our own personal relationships with God can be strengthened through prayer. This book addresses how to develop an effective personal prayer life as well as our responsibility to pray for others, which leads to a deeper purpose and understanding of prayer principles. James writes that the prayer of a righteous person is powerful and effective (James 5:6). You can have a powerful and effective prayer life.

We will explore five creeds in this prayer manifesto that illustrate why we pray and why we must be global-minded in our own prayer life. This is not a self-help book. You must acknowledge that all your strength and help come from God. This book outlines principles found in the Word of God. Ask the Holy Spirit, our helper, to give you wisdom, revelation, and understanding to apply the Word to your life.

> Father God, all of my help and strength come from you alone. Without you, I am unable to do anything. I am nothing without you. I have nothing apart from you. Your Word is a lamp unto my feet and a light unto my path. Thank you for your Holy Spirit, who strengthens me daily.

The beginning of Jesus's public ministry began when he read from the scroll of Isaiah. So began the fulfillment of his journey here on earth. Just as his journey began by reading from the scroll, so let your personal journey into a powerful, supernatural life of prayer begin. As you read this book, there will be scrolls along the way to guide you. Pay particular attention to them, and consider how you will begin fulfilling your own purpose as a global-minded prayer warrior.

Our Prayer Manifesto

Creed I: We believe God loves the world so much that he gave his best and highest gift, his Son, that we, as believers, would have the right to fellowship with God through prayer now and enjoy everlasting life with him forever.

Creed II: We believe that an effective personal prayer life is the foundation for our ability to pray for others.

Creed III: We believe that because God loves the world, it is our responsibility to pray for it.

Creed IV: We believe we have a special responsibility to pray for our local church as it fulfills the great commission in this world.

Creed V: We believe an effective personal prayer life coupled with our willingness to pray for others unleashes the supernatural power within us when we are faced with challenges and opposition.

Pray Now

Creed I

We believe God loves the world so much that he gave his best and highest gift, his Son, that we, as believers, would have the right to fellowship with God now through prayer and enjoy everlasting life with him forever.

Chapter 1

Why Should We Pray?

In this chapter, we will address two main topics: the reasons we pray and why taking control of our thoughts is a prerequisite to an effective prayer life where you experience answered prayers. About a year ago, I was reminded about the reasons we pray when I traveled with my family to Destin, Florida. As we drove from Memphis to Destin for spring break, a DVD cartoon about a superhero was playing in the car. Sitting in the front passenger seat, I was able to listen to only the dialogue of whatever movie was entertaining my children for the almost nine-hour drive. One of the main characters was complaining about the superhero: "We never had super villains until we had a superhero!"

As I listened to him complain about this superhero, I was reminded that we, God's beloved children, are superheroes, and that Jesus is the ultimate superhero. When we accepted Jesus Christ as our Lord and Savior, we were given access to supernatural strength as the Holy Spirit came to dwell in us. As God's dear children, we face some of our attacks because we *are* superheroes. Unlike this superhero, we wage spiritual battles. "For our struggle is not against flesh and blood, but against the rulers, against the authorities, against

3

the powers of this dark world and against the spiritual forces of evil in the heavenly realms" (Ephesians 6:12).

Jesus, the original "superhero," has already defeated the super villains. Our role is to have a working knowledge of how to walk in victory against these defeated spiritual villains. God said in Hosea 4:6 that his people perish because of a lack of knowledge. God has given us everything we need in order to gain the victory over any situation, and we cannot afford to be passive superheroes. Instead of just waiting for the attack, we must learn how to go on the offensive. The good news is that we are not in these battles alone. God is standing by, ready and willing to protect us from the onslaught of the villain. God is our defender, and he acts on our behalf to fight all our battles. He promised every believer that he would never leave or forsake him.

Whatever challenges you are facing today, God is with you. He knows how to protect you. The secret to obtaining the victory against any super villain lies in his Word. We have to get to know God's Word because when we know his Word, we know him. God promised us that we would be strong and carry out great exploits when we know him (Daniel 11:32). He also promised he would train our hands for the battles against the super villains (Psalm 144:1). God will teach us how to walk in victory.

Satan is the ultimate super villain, but he is limited in what he can do. When Satan went roaming back and forth looking for someone to unleash his super villains on, he found Job. Job was a God-fearing man. The Bible tells us Job was blameless and upright. Furthermore, he feared God and shunned evil (Job 1:1). Although God allowed everything Job had to be in Satan's control, God told him he could not kill Job. In Job 1:12, "The Lord said to Satan, 'Very well, then, everything he has is in your hands, but on the man himself do not lay a finger.' Then Satan went out from the presence of the Lord".

Unlike the reader, Job did not have this glimpse into what was happening in the spiritual realm. Job was ultimately able to triumph over the external attacks on his property and family—his own super villains—by trusting God.

The Enemy does not have free reign in our lives. God has the supreme authority over any super villain. So what is our role in the battle? God has given us his Word and a very specific role to play in gaining victory over our situations. We do not have to let the enemy run rampant in our lives. For this reason, we must have a God-centered approach in our battle against super villains. We are responsible for living a life of obedience and fellowship with God. By focusing our attention on God when we are challenged, we place our confidence in God's sovereign ability. We have the accounts of Job, Paul, and even Jesus as a testament of where our confidence should be when we face these attacks.

Secret Identity

Many of our favorite superheroes are disguised as regular people most of the time, but they are able to undergo some type of transformation as the situation presents. Many superheroes have a secret identity that is not apparent to those in the world around them—even their closest friends are unable to surmise their secret.

As a superhero, we also have a secret identity. Our secret identity—the real us—looks just like Jesus. When the Father looks at us, the image he sees is that of our big brother, Jesus—the ultimate superhero. Because of the indwelling of the Holy Spirit, we are being changed into the likeness of Christ. As a superhero, we must grow in knowledge of our true role and authority in this world in order to become more aware of our super strength. Why do we need super strength? We will face challenges in this world. We should not become afraid when we are challenged. "Finally, be strong in the Lord and in his mighty power. Put on the full armor of God so that you can take your stand against the Devil's schemes" (Ephesians 6:10–11).

It is not enough to say we are not of this world. We, as members of the body of Christ, must learn how to put on the full armor of God and be involved in this world in a positive way. There will be seasons in our life when the enemy sends his super villains to attack us. The good news, however, is that we already have the victory. God in his infinite ability and supernatural strength is always working on our behalf. "And we know that in all things God works for the good of those who love him, who have been called according to his purpose" (Romans 8:28). For this reason, our confidence, in any situation, should be in the Lord and in his sovereign ability to save us.

"The Lord is my light and my salvation—whom shall I fear? The Lord is the stronghold of my life—of whom shall I be afraid? When evil men advance against me to devour my flesh, when my enemies and my foes attack me, they will stumble and fall. Though an army besiege me, my heart will not fear; though war break out against me, even then will I be confident" (Psalm 27:1–3).

The Word Is Our Weapon

God's Word is our best supernatural weapon against super villains. A superhero must know how to use his supernatural weapon. Consider how Jesus chastised Peter in John 18:1–11 for trying to use natural weapons in response to the enemy's plan to kill him. The men showed up carrying weapons seeking to capture Jesus. Peter responded by drawing his own sword and attacking one of the men. Peter, unaware of what was really happening, was acting outside his authority and was interfering with God's plan. Where would we be had Peter been successful?

How useless our actions are when they are done outside the will of God! Our weapons are spiritual, and they are not the weapons of the world (2 Corinthians 10:4). God's Word, our weapon against the super villain's schemes, must be sown in our hearts. When we hang the Word of God around our neck (Proverbs 6:21), it will surface when we are faced with an attack from the enemy. In every situation, we are responsible for finding out what God has promised us in his Word. As a superhero, our role is to know the Word of God that applies to our situations. Once the Word is sown in our hearts, it will begin to permeate our thoughts and actions, which sets the stage for God to act against the villains on our behalf.

Supernatural GPS

The Word of God is your personal "GPS"—it tells you where you are headed. It does not dwell on where you are right now. Rather, its purpose is to give you the steps to get to where you need to go. Unlike the manmade GPS, the Word of God will never steer you wrong. We can steer ourselves wrong when we turn down the volume or simply ignore what it is telling us to do. What is the Word telling you to do now? It does not have to be something profound. Turn right in 50 feet. Turn left in 5 miles. Stay on this road for 186 miles. Often we get anxious or impatient and too soon turn off the path he has for us. I have learned that God, like the manmade GPS, gives us directions in small steps. First step, trust me. Second step, lean not unto your own understanding. Next, acknowledge me. Finally, I will direct your path (Proverbs 3:5–6). While it seems easier and more advantageous to jump to the second or third step, our obedience is imperative if we want to get to our destination. There are some things in our life that must be done sequentially. God is a God of order.

What if we looked the way superheroes do at some of the super villains who are trying to kill and destroy us? Without hesitation, the protagonist fights super villain after super villain, confident in his superhero DNA. Well, we have God's DNA, which is greater than anything in this world. In every episode there is a fight scene where it looks as though the superhero will lose. Just when it seems like the villain has won, the hero digs deep within himself and manages to land the death blow. The battle is over, and our superhero is victorious again.

While we want the victory in our lives, we often get discouraged when the enemy tries to attack us. Although the enemy knows he has ultimately been defeated, he will try to get in a few sucker punches if we lower our guard. Do not be discouraged. We should not allow the enemy to land blow after blow. He does not fight fair. But the truth is, neither do we! David proclaims in Psalm 18:29, "With your help, I can advance against a troop; with my God I can scale a wall". We are the original "wall scalers." We trample great lions and serpents! (Psalm 91:13). God has given us supernatural abilities that make it possible to defeat any villain we face. I hope you have come to recognize who you really are in Christ—a superhero, a "wall scaler."

Heading in the Right Direction

That spring break when we were driving to Destin, I really wanted to get there quicker. My then-five-year-old, Andrew, kept asking, "Where is the beach?" We were one hundred fifty miles outside Memphis—there was no beach. Aldon, his big brother, had to explain every hour that we were almost there! Andrew would look outside his window each time and ask, "Where is it now?" No matter how badly we all wanted to get to the beach, we had to drive through Mississippi and Alabama in order to get to Florida. No matter how many times I pressed the buttons on our Garmin GPS, the facts kept staring me in my face. If we had turned off 45 South too soon, we would not have arrived. Furthermore, if we had stopped and refused to go any farther, we would never have gotten to Destin. If we had taken a shortcut and gotten lost, we might not have arrived at our destination. We simply had to stay the course. We were either going to make it to the resort, or we were not. As we begin exploring our role as a superhero, we must realize there are no shortcuts. Our obedience to the Word of God and our fellowship with God are only achieved when we learn how to function in our role.

No matter where you are in your walk with God, it is not too late for you to learn how to use your supernatural weapons and operate as a superhero. Even if you have started to go your own way and have neglected your relationship with God, God waits patiently for you with open arms. Even if we ignore him and try our little shortcuts, our Father stands ready for us to turn back to him. No matter how off-course you become, he is still waiting for you. He is a loving God. Jesus went through so much for us so we could fellowship with God again. He loves to fellowship with us, and it pleases him when we want to be with him. If your life is headed in the wrong direction, or if you have just pulled over on the side of the road in your walk with God, perhaps you have not been serious about truly seeking his face and knowing his plan for your life. It is not too late. This book can be your first step. Let's make a U-turn. The enemy will get upset and may even throw a couple of rocks at your windshield. It doesn't matter!

Prayer for Wisdom When Reading This Book

> Father God, I was created to worship you and to fellowship with you. I praise you right now, Father, with all my heart, all my soul, and all my being. As I read this book, I pray you will speak to me and show me how to apply myself. Father, your Word in James says we are to ask for wisdom and that you would give it to us freely. I ask for wisdom, Father, concerning how to use prayer to unleash my supernatural power. I look forward to spending time with you as I explore your Word. Thank you, Father.

Chapter 2

Taking Authority of Your Thought Life

The lion is one of the most powerful mammals in the animal kingdom. When most people think of a lion, they imagine a strong, majestic, and fierce creature. Lions are carnivorous and often roam the land in search of food. Have you ever seen a video of a lion or lioness attacking its prey? It hunts by sneaking up on its prey and catching its victim off guard. The lion is capable of killing very large prey and can feast on it for hours. One of the ways it attacks is by enclosing the victim's mouth and nostrils in its massive jaws. The helpless animal is defenseless against this form of attack. Unable to call out to the herd for help, the animal's body is drained of its life, and the lion enjoys the fruits of its labor.

Consider this Scripture found in 1 Peter 5:8: "Be alert and of sober mind. Your enemy the Devil prowls around like a roaring lion looking for someone to devour". How interesting that God would compare a lion to the enemy. Unlike the king of the jungle, however, the enemy is already defeated! "My God sent his angel, and he shut the mouths of the lions. They have not hurt me, because I was found innocent in his sight. Nor have I ever done any wrong before you, O king" (Daniel 6:22).

There are two important messages in the Scripture found in 1 Peter.

First we learn the enemy is, in fact, looking to devour us. I instantly think of the image of the lion attacking its prey. When we are under attack, our first response is to start imagining that something bad is about to happen. More importantly, we allow the enemy to silence us with his roars and these negative imaginations. Instead of using our voice to pray to our heavenly Father, we are silenced and cannot find the strength to gain the victory over the situation. Sometimes we hide from sharing with our friends, or we shrink back from attending church. This must stop! Cry out to God for help. Let the "herd" know you are in trouble.

Second, one of the methods the enemy uses to try to attack us is by roaring. Oftentimes we allow fear to enter our hearts because we hear the roar of the lion. We allow our imaginations to take over and cause us to react in fear based on the sound of the lion's roar. How many times have you been overcome with fear and anxiety because of some news that was shared with you? Perhaps it was merely the threat of something bad that sent you into fear mode. The enemy's goal is to bombard our thoughts with images or ideas that paralyze us and make us useless. *The enemy wants to silence and paralyze you.*

Why is our thought life so important? The majority of the battle is in our mind. We are to take a stand against arguments, theories, and other thoughts that challenge the Word of God (2 Corinthians 10:5). "We demolish arguments and every pretension that sets itself up against the knowledge of God, and we take captive every thought to make it obedient to Christ. And we will be ready to punish every act of disobedience, once your obedience is complete" 2 Corinthians 10:5–6.

Here Paul tells us three main things about ungodly thoughts. *First* you learn that you have the responsibility and authority to control your thoughts. How many times have you allowed negative images or thoughts to run free in your mind? Before you know it, your mind has been gripped with fear. This does not have to be the case. God has equipped you with the ability to control your thought life. *Second*, Paul writes that proud and ungodly thoughts try to challenge the veracity of God's Word in your life. These thoughts are a direct threat to the truth found in the Word of God. All wisdom comes from God, and he alone is the author of truth. Allowing your mind to meditate on negative thoughts actually gives the enemy a place to roam in your life. Give God first place in your thought life. The Word of God should not have to compete with ungodly or sinful thoughts. *Third*, Paul writes in Corinthians that these negative and unscriptural thoughts lead to disobedience. This is why your prayer life is so important. When these thoughts challenge the Word of God's power in your life, pray as Luke instructs us. Pray that you would be enabled to speak boldly what God's Word proclaims about that situation (Acts 4:29).

The Power of Speaking

Let's look at one of my favorite examples of how powerful the process of speaking can be. Try this: without saying anything, start at one hundred and count backward to ninety in your mind. Just think it without saying a word. Go! Okay, now start at ninety and count backward to eighty, but this time open your mouth and begin reciting your ABCs at the same time. Go! Can you do both at the same time? Think about it. Are you able to count backward in your mind while reciting the ABCs? No. Why not? Is it because you do not know your ABCs, or perhaps one hundred is too big a number? Absolutely not! The truth lies in the fact that the process of speaking is so powerful. Speaking requires the full effort of your mind—the battleground.

Similarly, when negative thoughts or imaginations enter your mind, instantly open your mouth and begin to say the Scripture or promise that this ungodly thought is trying to challenge. Later we will talk about prayer/Scripture cards, which can prove invaluable until you begin to memorize Scriptures to use. You have control over these thoughts, and unleashing the power of prayer will strengthen and empower you to live the life God has in store for you. God never promised you there would not be challenges or that these thoughts would not come; rather, he has given you the power to gain victory over them.

The Power of Meditation

Speaking the Word is only part of the solution. Speaking is the first step toward taking authority over your thoughts. Meditation is the second and probably most important step in maintaining a healthy thought pattern. Meditation is defined as "discourse intended to guide others in contemplation" (*Merriam-Webster.com*). I have included Scriptures throughout the book so you can meditate on them or contemplate about them as you process the shared information. I heard a pastor say meditations are creative imaginations. No matter how creatively you can imagine, God wants to blow your mind!

The Message Bible translation should make this even more lucid: "God can do anything, you know—far more than you could ever imagine or guess or request in your wildest dreams! He does it not by pushing us around but by working within us, his Spirit deeply and gently within us. Glory to God in the church! Glory to God in the Messiah, in Jesus! Glory down all the generations! Glory through all millennia! Oh, yes!" Ephesians 3:20.

Meditating Day and Night

Many of your negative thoughts have roamed unchecked in your mind for years, maybe even decades. Some of your most deeply rooted thoughts may have been formed before you became a believer. Do not be discouraged by this. There is hope and you can gain authority. Revelation is progressive—it does not happen over night.

You must be committed to replacing your ungodly thoughts or ideas with godly thoughts. How can you do this?

Meditation involves three action steps. Let's look at what the Psalmist says about meditation: "Blessed is the man who does not walk in the counsel of the wicked or stand in the way of sinners or sit in the seat of mockers. But his delight is in the law of the Lord, and on his law he meditates day and night" (Psalm 1:1–2).

Step 1: Walk

Decide from whom you will receive your counsel. Will you follow the counsel of God as revealed in his Word, or will you follow the world's advice or understanding? As you begin taking authority of your thoughts, you need to feed your mind with the Word. Books, audiotapes, and even music may be helpful as you learn more about God's wisdom and how to walk according to his counsel.

Step 2: Stand

Surround yourself with others who also speak and meditate on the Word of God. Standing also means you do not follow the same path as someone who is sinful. You cannot continue in the life of sin from which you were redeemed. Make a decision to live for Christ. If you mess up, ask for forgiveness and turn away from the sin.

Step 3: Sit

Do not adopt the ways of people you may encounter who mock or deride the Word of God or challenge its veracity. You may find yourself surrounded by people who may ask about this new attitude you have adopted. They may try to laugh at you and make you believe all of *that* is not necessary. It's not necessary to go to church *every* Sunday. It's not necessary to pray *all* the time. Do you really have to stop doing (you insert the activity) to be a believer?

Do not adopt their ways. You have made a decision to sow righteousness and faithfulness in the things of God. What harvest can you expect in return? Answer: blessings and a deeper fellowship with God.

Imagining is a form of meditation. It involves feeding your mind with godly thoughts or images. Just as the enemy would like to fill your mind with negative thoughts, you should spend time sending positive, godly thoughts to your mind. Let's practice this form of meditating. When you lie in your bed right before you go to sleep, imagine what God's Word would look like fully manifested in your circumstance. Try it before you go to bed tonight. During your wait time when you pray, ask God to show you pictures or glimpses—creative imaginings—of what he has for you. This is a good way to spend time waiting for God to speak to you. This can be an important step in the renewal process. Many of you are facing situations so challenging you might struggle with imagining what your life would be like otherwise. Imagine what it would be like if you had money left at the end of the month after you paid your bills. What does it look like to not have to use the nebulizer on your asthmatic child again? How would you feel being able to go on that missionary trip after all? What does not arguing with your spouse about *that* issue look like? Make this part of your nightly prayer time.

Prayer Is Fellowship with God

You ask, Why is prayer so important? Prayer is not merely about defeating the enemy and overcoming attacks or struggles. Prayer is about fellowshipping with your heavenly Father. Prayer means talking with and listening to God. Prayer is an essential element in your walk with God, and so important is this fellowship that God sent his only Son as a sacrifice for your sins to enable you the opportunity to enjoy his presence. God has called you to live significant and victorious lives.

The key to victory, however, lies in your relationship with God. Know that when you pray, you are talking directly to God. Therefore, you should approach the throne of grace with confidence knowing your heavenly Father hears you (Hebrews 4:16).

In *The Prayer Manifesto for the Globally Conscious*, you will learn how to cultivate a healthy relationship with God through a strong prayer life. Let's be silent no more!

Before we move on to the next chapter, let's pray you will take authority over your thought life and enjoy the kind of relationship with God that you were created to enjoy. Some of the information shared in this book may be new to you, or it may reaffirm some principles and practices that you have already established in your prayer life. Regardless of your background, it is important that you begin this journey with an open mind and heart to hear from God.

Prayer for Taking Authority of Your Thought Life

Father, as I begin this journey to a deeper prayer life with you, I declare that you are faithful in my life. I sing praises to you. There is no one like you. There is no one before you. You are God alone in every area of my life. You are sovereign. You are my provider. You are my deliverer. You stoop down and you rescue me when I call you. We demolish arguments and every pretension that sets itself up against the knowledge of God, and we take captive every thought to make it obedient to Christ (2 Corinthians 10:5). Thank you, Father, for giving me the authority to take captive every thought that challenges what I know to be true in your Word. I know that you are for me and not against me. I know that you have good plans for me and that you love me. I grab hold of every thought that tries to enter my mind and tries to harm, kill, or destroy what you have said in your Word. I rebuke every thought that you did not give me. I rebuke every thought that does not line up with your Word. I love you, Lord. Thank you for your Son, Jesus. Because of what Jesus did, I can take authority over these thoughts.

The First Scroll

God has given us everything that we need in order to gain the victory over any situation, and we cannot afford to be passive superheroes.

As a superhero, we must grow in knowledge of our true role and authority in this world in order to become more aware of our super strength.

When we hang the Word of God around our neck (Proverbs 6:21), it will surface when we are faced with an attack from the enemy.

We are to take a stand against arguments, theories, and other thoughts that challenge the word of God (2 Corinthians 10:5).

Speaking requires the full effort of your mind- the battle ground.

During your wait time when you pray, ask God to show you pictures or glimpses- creative imaginings- of what he has for you.

Prayer means talking with and listening to God.

Seven Tips for an Effective Personal Prayer Life

Creed II

We believe an effective personal prayer life is the foundation for our ability to pray for others.

Chapter 3

First Tip: Begin Your Prayer with Worship

Worship refers to the actions we take and attitudes we have when praising God for who he is and thanking him for what he has done. You worship God with your actions, which include what you are saying or doing, and your attitude, which is in humility and reverence to God's greatness. Whether you use one sentence to thank God or spend twenty minutes in his presence in worship, you should begin your prayer time with worship. Making a commitment to worship is the first component to establishing a prayer life and is essential in cultivating a relationship with God. Prayer should flow out of your worship time. Having an attitude of thanksgiving and praise allows you to have a more God-centered prayer instead of always having a needs-centered prayer. During this time of worship, you should express how much you appreciate and love him. Sometimes you may cite specific instances in your life that you are thanking him for, or you may use your own words to talk with him about how awesome he is.

Whatever you choose, be sure your worship does not focus on your feelings. In fact, when you clear the clutter from your mind and ignore how you "feel" and really concentrate on his greatness, you acknowledge that God is greater than any feeling, emotion, situation, or obstacle in your life. Sometimes we focus so much attention on our situation and what we want to ask God that we forget God is awesome and worthy of our praise and gratitude for what he has already done. Worship him regardless of what you are experiencing or how desperate you feel.

Who Is God?

Worshipping God means you have an appreciation for who he is. The Bible gives us glimpses into who God is through his character, in ways to address him, and the role he plays in our lives. An understanding of the character of God and the roles he wants to have in our lives will help us understand how invaluable a relationship with him is. It will also help us focus on him for who he is when we are tempted to see our situation as insurmountable. A healthy prayer life is fundamental in our quest for a deeper relationship with him.

Let's look at partial list of the names of God as adapted from Strong's *Exhaustive Concordance of the Bible* as we learn how to pray with a God-centered focus (all translations are from the New International Version of the Bible):

- God: Genesis 14:18–20: "Blessed be Abram by God Most High"
- The Faithful God: Deuteronomy 7:9: "He is the faithful God."
- The God of Truth: Psalm 31:5: "redeem me, O Lord, the God of truth."
- The God that Heals: Exodus 15:26: "for I am the Lord, who heals you."

- The Righteous God: Isaiah 45:21: "a righteous God and a Savior; there is none but me."
- The Almighty God: Genesis 17:1:"I am God Almighty."
- The Most High God: Psalm 9:2: "I will sing praise to your name, O Most High."
- The Everlasting God: Psalm 90:1–2: "from everlasting to everlasting you are God."
- The God who sees me: Genesis 16:13: "You are the God who sees me."
- The Mighty God: Isaiah 9:6:"Wonderful Counselor, Mighty God, Everlasting Father, Prince of Peace."
- The God of knowledge: 1 Samuel 2:3: "for the Lord is a God who knows."
- The Great God: Deuteronomy 10:17: "the great God, mighty and awesome."
- The God of Glory: Psalm 29:3: "the God of glory thunders."
- The Holy God: Isaiah 5:16: "the holy God will show himself holy by his righteousness."
- The God of the Heavens: Psalm 136:26: "Give thanks to the God of heaven."
- The God of my life: Psalm 42:8: "the God of my life…"
- The Gracious God: Jonah 4:2: "you are a gracious and compassionate God."
- The God of Israel: Psalm 68:35: "the God of Israel."
- The God of my strength: Psalm 42:9: "God my Rock."
- The God of Endurance and Consolation: Romans 15:5: "the God who gives endurance and encouragement."
- The God of Compassion: Deuteronomy 4:31: "For the Lord your God is a merciful God."
- All Merciful God: Nehemiah 9:31: "for you are a gracious and merciful God"

- The God of my salvation: Isaiah 12:2: "Surely God is my salvation."
- The Jealous God: Exodus 20:5: "for I, the Lord your God, am a jealous God."
- The Awesome God: Nehemiah 9:32: "O our God, the great, mighty and awesome God."

When you pray, remember these names and use them to frame your worship time. Ann Spangler has written the wonderful *Praying the Names of God: A Daily Guide,* about how to pray daily the names of God. I encourage you to read it. While you do not need to use any religious language when you worship, reflecting on God's character as revealed to us through his names will help us stay God-centered in our worship time. If you are still unsure about what to say, just thank God for what he has done (Psalm 69:30). Sing to him (Psalm 95:2). Whatever you decide, do it with gladness and joyful words (Psalm 100:2). Let your worship time be sincere, and do not be afraid to get excited and passionate in your worship (Hebrews 12:28).

Prayer of Praise

> It is good to praise the Lord and make music to his name, O Most High. I proclaim your love in the morning and your faithfulness at night. Father, as I wake up this morning/prepare for bed tonight, I declare you are faithful in my life. I sing praises to you this morning/evening. I am thankful for who you are in my life, and I stand in reverence and awe of your great power. You are a consuming fire, and I am glad you are in my life. I praise your name. I bless you with all my heart, soul, and mind. I thank you for this day that you have made.

Chapter 4

Second Tip: Conduct an Examination of Your Attitudes and Actions

It is always good to pray the Holy Spirit will lead you at a time of self-examination. During this time in your prayer, you are asking the Holy Spirit to reveal any areas of your life where you hold prejudices or carry attitudes that might affect your ability to pray for others or extend the love of Christ "to all nations" (Matthew 28:19). You want to honor the Father with your lips and your heart. Ask God to show you if your heart is far from him. Later, you will explore the importance of having compassion for God's people, but you may want to ask God now if you have lost your sense of compassion or have become numb to the circumstances that people are facing. You do not want to become so entrenched in your local church body that you lose the ability to relate to those God may need you to witness. Having a judgmental spirit will inhibit your ability to go make disciples of all nations. We do not want to regard ourselves as being better than those around us.

If you find any of these attitudes prevalent, ask for forgiveness. Oftentimes we struggle worshipping God because we have "unchecked" thoughts or motives. If you are led to repent about something when you first start to pray, then repent! You will find it easier to move into worship if you acknowledge where you may have fallen short and ask for forgiveness. Do not let sin keep you from entering his presence. God is faithful and promises to always be there for us. He tells us nothing can separate us from his love. You do not have to wait until your prayer time to ask for forgiveness! If the Holy Spirit is leading you to apologize to someone or ask for forgiveness, quickly obey. True repentance not only involves confession of sin, it includes a decision to turn your back on whatever you were doing, thinking, or saying that caused you to sin. You must be willing to completely abandon the sin and make a conscious effort to not return to it! Ask God to help you in this area. For now, however, ask God to forgive you and then press on!

After you have examined your attitude, ask God for more love because

- Love covers a multitude of sins.
- Love casts out fear.
- Love does no harm to its neighbor.
- Love is patient and kind.
- Love is humble.
- Love forgives.
- Love compels us to action.

Having a Humble Spirit

As members of the body of Christ, you are instructed to humble yourself and serve God with gladness (Psalm 100:2). You are not to be glad because of what you have, rather you are to be glad with where you are spiritually. Consider these Scriptures from the King James Bible regarding humility:

"My soul shall make her boast in the Lord: the humble shall hear thereof, and be glad" (Psalm 34:2).

"Pride goeth before destruction, and a haughty spirit before a fall. Better is it to be of a humble spirit with the lowly than to divide the spoil with the proud" (Proverbs 16:18–19).

"Whosoever therefore shall humble himself as this little child, the same is greatest in the kingdom of heaven" (Matthew 18:4).

"Humble yourself under the mighty hand of God that he may exalt you in due time" (I Peter 5:6).

"Consider this in your heart: the wise will hear, receive, and increase the years of your life" (Proverbs 4:10–13).

This requires humility. There are two ingredients for humility.

First you must make a decision to lower your will, and then you must follow through. Your will is the place in your soul where decisions are made, learned behavior is promoted, and desire is kindled. It is the seat of your feelings and character. Your willpower is strong. God has given you the power to set your own will and choose between life and death (Proverbs 18: 21). Hence, you are in control of your own will. You must humbly submit your will to God's will. Moreover, being humble requires that you do something. You must lower yourself in your own estimation.

Consider how David humbled himself before Saul: "And David said unto Saul, Who am I? And what is my life, or my father's family in Israel? And my family the least of all the families of the tribe of Benjamin? Wherefore then speakest thou so to me?" (I Samuel 9: 21, KJV).

The second ingredient of humility is embracing the wisdom of God that you are receiving. Being humble allows your heart to be open to hear wisdom's voice (Proverbs 11:2). This wisdom could come in the form of instruction or discipline from your pastor. When you humble yourself and submit to God, you are lowering your will in order to receive God's will.

Humility, however, is not to be confused with passivity. You must put your plans to the side and actively accept God's plan for your life. There is no such thing as partial obedience. When Jesus humbled himself and submitted to God's will, he prayed that God's will be done in his life and declared his own will would not be done (Matthew 26:39). We must follow Jesus's example.

Prayer of Forgiveness

"Who can discern his errors? Forgive my hidden faults. Keep your servant also from willful sins; may they not rule over me. Then will I be blameless, innocent of great transgression. May the words of my mouth and the meditation of my heart be pleasing in your sight, O Lord, my rock and my redeemer" (Psalm 19:12–14). Father, as I stand in your presence, I ask you to forgive me of any sin or hidden fault in my life. Show me how to love you, Father. Keep me from committing willful sin because I know you are perfect. Father, I know sin causes me to turn my back on you. I need you and cannot go through this day without you. I repent from any sin in my life and turn away from things that do not please you. May sin not rule over me. I am free to worship you and praise you. I will watch what I say and the thoughts and intentions of my heart. May the words that I say please you. May the intentions I have when I act please you. I love you and need you this day. Amen.

After you have been in this process for a while, you may begin to feel as if you have nothing to confess when you go before the Lord in prayer. At that point, just spend time listening to the Holy Spirit. Perhaps he will share something with you that you did not know was a sin. The Holy Spirit convicts us of sins, but he does not condemn us

(Romans 8:1–4). Do not become discouraged because those feelings of inferiority will try to keep you from serving God. Remember, the enemy wants to silence you and does not want you to go to God in prayer. Colossians 3:13 reminds us to forgive each other, whoever has a complaint against anyone, just as the Lord forgave us. You are forgiven!

Chapter 5

Third Tip: Pray with the Word of God

Jesus has given us a pattern to teach us how to pray (Luke 11:1–4). Let's look at his example: "And he said to them, when you pray, say: Our Father who is in heaven, hallowed be your name, your kingdom come, your will be done held holy and revered on earth as it is in heaven. Give us daily our bread food for the morrow, and forgive us our sins, for we ourselves also forgive everyone who is indebted to us who has offended us or done us wrong. And bring us not into temptation but rescue us from evil" (Amplified Bible).

Following Jesus's example, we learn our prayer must be for the Father's will to be done, held holy and revered on earth just as it is done in heaven. This means our prayers should line up with what the Father has already revealed to us, especially in his Word, the Bible.

So how do you know if what you are praying lines up with the Word of God? Go to the Bible and look for two or three scriptural references for your situation. We will later discuss how to do this. Remind yourself that you serve a God who is able to do immeasurably more than all you ask or imagine (Ephesians 3:20). Do not limit yourself to praying for problem situations to stop being problems. Always pray the Scripture in a positive way. For example, if there is someone in your life you are praying would receive salvation, also pray that he or she would become actively involved in the church and would be able to lead others to Christ. Your prayers should incorporate your praying the Word of God back to him and reminding him of his promises.

My mother has made it her responsibility to teach my sons how to pray with Scriptures. She has a very detailed strategy—one that I remember from my own childhood. First they had to learn the twenty-third psalm. Then they had to learn to pray for their family—and extended family. When they could recite all of this in its entirety from memory, she made them start praying for people or for certain things using their own words. She wanted them to understand that they should always use Scriptures when they pray, so she made this part of the process. I do not think they will ever forget how to do this. I know I haven't!

Using Prayer/Scripture Cards

The easiest way for me to use Scriptures when I pray is through the use of prayer or Scripture cards. I keep a set of index-sized, laminated cards with me on a ring that I can pull out whenever I need to pray. These cards contain Scriptures or prayers about specific topics, or they may contain actual prayers about situations. For example, I have Scripture cards that contain Scriptures I frequently use when praying for my husband or children.

If you are one of those people who is gifted with an ability to memorize vast amounts of information, like my son, Aldon, then you may want to commit to memorizing a few choice Scriptures that are applicable to many of our daily challenges. I am amazed at how quickly Aldon can memorize huge amounts of text. The beauty in his talent is that he remembers the information later! If only he could remember all of his homework assignments. I guess you remember what you want to remember. If you are not like Aldon, then Scripture cards are the way to go.

I find that the cards serve two purposes. First, they are a quick reference to Scriptures or prayers that I have assimilated by topic. Second, because they are always with me, they remind me of the need to pray all the time! When I am praying for the strength to forgive someone who has wronged me, I pull out the cards that I have organized on forgiveness. What's neat about my forgiveness cards is that they start off reminding me of the fact I have been forgiven and that I too have wronged others—directly or indirectly—because of my actions. Then there are Scriptures that walk me through the process of forgiving that other person. How many times have you prayed about someone who wronged you without any recognition of the truth that you have also committed wrongs against God? The prayer cards keep me honest too! Without the reminder of my own humanity, it would be easy for me to only focus on the other person. I am not sure if I could do that as easily in the heat of the moment.

How do you know which Scriptures apply to your situation? Use a concordance! Most Bibles come with a concordance. *Strong's Concordance* is probably one of the better known editions. A good concordance can help you find Scriptures for a specific topic. We will discuss this process later in greater detail.

When You Fast

Sometimes when you pray, it may require you to fast. Ask God to give you the ability to discern when what you are praying requires prayer and fasting. Matthew 6:16 tells us that when we fast, we should not look somber as the hypocrites do, because they look a certain way so that people know that they are fasting. Notice it does not read "if you fast," rather it says when you fast. Jentezen Franklin's book *Fasting: Opening the Door to a Deeper, More Intimate, More Powerful Relationship with God* is an excellent resource for more information on fasting and the role of fasting in our prayer life. I encourage you to read it to gain a deeper understanding of how important fasting is in our walk with God.

Speaking in Your Heavenly Language

One of the most controversial gifts of the Holy Spirit is speaking in tongues. While speaking in tongues is not required for salvation, there are many reasons a believer should desire manifestation of this gift. Any discussion on prayer should also include a discussion on praying or speaking in tongues. Consider the following reasons for praying in tongues.

Edifying Your Spirit

"He who speaks in a tongue edifies himself, but he who prophesies edifies the church" (1 Corinthians 14:4).

Building Your Faith

"But you, dear friends, build yourselves up in your most holy faith and pray in the Holy Spirit" (Jude 1:20).

Speaking Divine Mysteries

"For anyone who speaks in a tongue does not speak to men but to God. Indeed, no one understands him; he utters mysteries with his spirit" (1 Corinthians 14:2)

Magnifying God

"For they heard them speaking in tongues and praising God" (Acts 10:46).

Praying the Will of God

"In the same way, the Spirit helps us in our weakness. We do not know what we ought to pray for, but the Spirit himself intercedes for us with groans that words cannot express. And he who searches our hearts knows the mind of the Spirit because the Spirit intercedes for the saints in accordance with God's will" (Romans 8:26–27).

A Sign to Unbelievers

"Tongues, then, are a sign, not for believers but for unbelievers; prophecy, however, is for believers, not for unbelievers" (1 Corinthians 14:22).

"And these signs will accompany those who believe: In my name they will drive out demons; they will speak in new tongues" (Mark 16:17).

If you are interested in more information about speaking in tongues, read the preceding Scriptures and ask the Holy Spirit to give you wisdom concerning an interpretation of the reasons for speaking in tongues. There is a public and private side to speaking in tongues, and many believers have been turned off when they do not understand the gift of speaking in tongues. While you are continuing to cultivate your relationship with God, open your heart to the understanding, wisdom, and trust that God is faithful and just and will complete the work he has begun in you. Your prayers should always be in line with what is in God's Word. You should pray that your prayer life and your natural life will line up to what he has said in his Word.

Prayer for Situations to Line up with God's Word

"As the rain and the snow come down from heaven, and do not return to it without watering the earth and making it bud and flourish, so that it yields seed for the sower and bread for the eater, so is my word that goes out from my mouth: It will not return to me empty, but will accomplish what I desire and achieve the purpose for which I sent it. You will go out in joy and be led forth in peace; the mountains and hills will burst into song before you, and all the trees of the field will clap their hands. Instead of the thorn bush will grow the pine tree, and instead of briers the myrtle will grow. This will be for the Lord's renown, for an everlasting sign, which will not be destroyed" (Isaiah 55:10–13).

Father, I thank you that your Word accomplishes all that it is intended to accomplish in my life. I praise you because when I speak your Word over my situation, it does not return to you empty. Your Word will return to you as a testimony of your faithfulness in my life. It achieves its purpose in my life. I declare that I will continually confess your Word over my situation until it achieves the purpose for which you have sent it. I further declare that I will go out in joy and will be led in peace. I will have a pine tree and not thorn bushes. Myrtle will grow in my life in this situation, not briars. You are faithful. You are Holy. You are all powerful. I confess boldly that my situation must line up to your Word right now!

Chapter 6

Fourth Tip: Pray Continually

We should pray continually (1 Thessalonians 5:17). James 5:16–18 assures us that the prayer of a righteous man (or woman) is powerful and effective! If you truly want to be effective in prayer, then pray continually! What does "continually" mean? To continue means to never cease doing something, but it also means to forge ahead through something. Most of us are used to thinking about praying continually as it relates to praying throughout the day, but let's look at both aspects of praying continually.

When you "never cease" to pray, that means you are praying throughout the day. Remember, God has promised to never leave us, and we must use our faith to believe that he hears us when we pray. For this reason, as you go through your normal day's activities, talk to God. Spend time on your lunch break talking with him. The prayer cards I mentioned earlier can be a fundamental resource for you as you learn how to pray throughout the day. While many of you may not have time to spend countless hours praying, you can spend two minutes at your desk between calls, or take thirty seconds to read a Scripture before getting out of the car to go to a meeting, or say a silent pray in your mind while the baby is napping. Look for opportunities throughout your day when you can sneak away and spend time talking with God. As we discussed earlier, you do not need to use any religious language, and you do not need to remember any Scriptures if you just want to talk with him. Tell God about your day and what is on your mind. Then take time to listen to him and hear his heart. You do not need to get on bended knee in the closet of your office to pray to God—although you can if you need to! I am amazed at how many people laugh at me when they see me talking in the car and no one is there with me. In this day and age of hands-free devices, I definitely do not look as weird as I used to, but I do not care!

The second part of praying continually means forging ahead through something. "Forging ahead" means you keep moving to the end regardless of the opposition you may encounter. It means continuing to pray about a situation until you see change. You do not want to pray a "one and done" prayer with the feeling that you may never have to pray about that situation again. Some situations or obstacles may require you to pray and fast daily for a period of time. This is part of what is meant by praying continually. Praying continually about something does not mean God did not hear you the first time, or that you need to beg him over and over to answer you. Rather, there will be some challenges that require you to show a faithful commitment to the end. You should always finish your prayer with the expectation that something will happen, but there will be times when you have to be persistent and continue to pray. Paul tells us in Colossians 4:2-6 to "be earnest and unwearied and steadfast in your prayer life, being both alert and intent in your praying with thanksgiving" (AMP).

Why do we not always get immediate answers to our prayers? Sometimes they may be selfish prayers, which James reminds us God does not answer: "When you ask, you do not receive, because you ask with wrong motives, that you may spend what you get on your pleasures" (James 4:3).

There may be instances where the enemy may be trying to hinder God's work in your life, and the answers to your prayers come slower than you think they should. Rest assured, however, God is sovereign and in control. Other times you may need to have faith that God hears you while you continue to be faithful until you receive your answer. Just as Elijah did not get discouraged when he was praying for rain, we are not to become discouraged and give up until we receive our answer (I Kings 18:30–46)!

Chapter 7

Fifth Tip: Take Time to Listen to the Father

This is probably the most unpracticed step in personal prayer. It was the hardest part of prayer for me—and it still is! I enjoy worshipping God and found it relatively easy when I first started praying. I also have an easy time using the concordance to find scriptural references about my situation. The problem, however, is that I cannot keep my mouth closed long enough to listen. Those who know me know I am never at a loss for words. Listening is definitely a growth area of mine! But this is one of the most important steps! What kind of relationship would you have with someone who talked the entire time and never listened to what you had to say? How often would you want to spend time with this person? Well, unlike us, God always wants to spend time with us and always has something to share with us.

Listening to God means recognizing his voice when he speaks to you. John reminds us that we are to hear and listen to God's voice, and because we hear and are listening, we will follow him (John 10:27).

How do you listen to God? God uses his Word, his Holy Spirit, his people, and occasionally events and experiences in our lives. God does not contradict himself or decide to do something in opposition with his Word. None of these forms of communication should be in conflict with one another. The Bible contains the answer key for every situation in your life. For this reason, you should always examine everything as it relates to Scripture—and not just one Scripture but at least two or three (Deuteronomy 19:15). John reminds us the Holy Spirit will guide us into all truth (John 16:13), and there are many illustrations in the Scriptures of how God used people to communicate with each other (Galatians 6:1–2). In Matthew 7:11, we see that God gives good gifts to his children. These good gifts communicate to us God's faithfulness and his everlasting love.

Sometimes the events that happen in our lives communicate God's displeasure with our disobedience. Consider the story of Jonah, where God clearly instructs Jonah to go to Nineveh and admonish the people so they could repent. Jonah did not want to and instead ran away. God allowed Jonah to be trapped in the belly of a huge fish until he prayed and asked for forgiveness (Jonah 1:17). This event, which was painful for Jonah, communicated to Jonah that God was not pleased with his disobedience and what God expected him to do.

Learning how to recognize and listen to God's voice requires a commitment on our behalf to hear him and the humility to obey what he is saying.

Chapter 8

Sixth Tip: Establish Prayer Partners

There are times when it is better to pray alone and other times when you need someone to pray with you. Prayer partnerships are an important component of an effective prayer experience. Consider this Scripture taken from Ecclesiastes 4:9–12: "Two are better than one because they have a good return for their labor: if either of them falls down, one can help the other up. But pity anyone who falls and has no one to help him up. Also, if two lie down together, they will keep warm. But how can one keep warm alone? Though one may be overpowered, two can defend themselves. A cord of three strands is not quickly broken". Therefore, God has established a framework for prayer partnerships.

How Do You Choose a Prayer Partner?

A prayer partnership is not the same thing as serving on the prayer ministry at a local church, which we will discuss later. Prayer partnerships may consist of a group of two or three believers who pray together at regular times, or as needed. They may elect to meet once a week (either in person or over the phone) or once a month. Consistency is the key in any relationship. It is no different in a prayer partnership. When establishing prayer partnerships, it is best to have a set time each week or month that you all agree to meet or talk over the telephone. Prayer partner relationships help remind us that prayer is about the experience. It is not a weekly event, it is about spending time with your partners. The roles of each member may change from season to season. Someone may serve as a coach, someone else may be more of a leader or facilitator, while another partner may really enjoy leading your worship time together. Regardless of the roles, allow the relationships to form, and be patient with one another as you learn to pray unselfishly for each other. Initially you may feel uneasy sharing your personal information. While this can be a challenge, do not let it hinder you. Start slowly, sharing less personal prayer requests, and as you build the relationships, you can get more personal. Plan to start off with a small amount of prayer time, say five to fifteen minutes, and then extend the time as you are faithful in coming together to pray.

There are two ingredients to establishing an effective prayer partnership. First, prayer partners are not necessarily a group of your friends. Ideally, your prayer partners are people who may attend your local church. Many effective partnerships, however, can be those between members of different churches. What is important is that they belong to the same household of faith. In addition, they should be people who know how to agree and intercede on your behalf. A prayer partner should be nonjudgmental and be someone who can keep the information confidential. The reason your friends may not be the best candidates is that they tend to bring their own biases, knowledge, and experiences about you to the prayer partnership. They know were the bodies are buried, so to speak, and might be tempted to periodically remind you of this. This does not mean your friends cannot pray for you. Tanyze has always been good at selecting Godly friends, but she knows who to go to when it's time to pray. Rather, a prayer partner is someone whose main purpose for being in a relationship with you is to pray for you.

Similarly, when I think about my grandmother and her prayer partner, Ms. Tillman, I remember the 7:00 a.m. phone calls. Ms. Tillman called faithfully every morning except Sundays. My grandmother was a woman of mighty faith who prayed all the time. She did not pray every day with her sisters, although they talked daily. Somewhere in her walk she realized her friend would be the perfect prayer partner. She did pray with her sisters, but her prayer partner had a different function in her prayer life.

The second ingredient to establishing an effective prayer partnership involves learning how to unselfishly pray for someone else. You should spend some time before you actually pray to decide what the focus of the prayer time will be. You may have an agenda already formed in your mind about what you want to ask the others to pray for, but when you meet you realize there is someone else who may have a more dire need but would take up the bulk of your time together. So what do you do? Do you continue with your own agenda, or do you unselfishly commit to focusing on the other person? Is there someone in the group who is facing a potentially debilitating situation? Then that may be the focus of that meeting or telephone call. Or perhaps you all agree to focus on praying for relationships or the community. Whatever the topic, be sure to keep the focus relevant and scriptural. Have your Scripture cards or bibles ready when you begin.

The ABCs of Praying Together

When you pray together, practice your ABCs.

A: *attentive.* Listen patiently and stay focused on the person who is talking or praying. Do not allow your mind to wander.

B: *biting your tongue.* This means you resist the initial temptation to start sharing your opinion or thoughts on what you just heard. Many of you have varied experiences and knowledge, but you have to be careful not to speak from your experiences unless you are sure the information you are sharing aligns with what the Word is saying about that situation.

C: *confer*. Always confer with Scripture. Together you all should think about which Scriptures apply to the situation. Pray about the situation or obstacle using the Word of God.

Chapter 9

Seventh Tip: Connect with a Local Church Body

There are many reasons a believer should regularly attend church and be connected with a local church body. For our discussion here, I would like for us to look at three main reasons.

Reason one: Matthew reminds us the church's main mission is to promote the gospel (Matthew 28:19). Your attendance and faithful contributions help support the church's outreach efforts in the community. Church outreach is fundamental to our ability to make disciples of all nations. The church does not exist to serve only those who regularly attend. Rather, there should be tangible and consistent exemplars of how your local church is impacting the community in which it is planted. In addition, your connection with a local church community means you are connecting the resources and talents that you bring to that local body so that the church can continue to work in the community. You have the hands and feet necessary to continue spreading the good news throughout your community, the nation, and even the world. When you attend church, you also receive regular instruction on how to live that is both motivating and encouraging. This should empower you to be able to share the gospel with others when you leave the church.

Reason two: When you connect with a local church body, you learn how to love and encourage one another. You have an expectation to do good for all people, especially those who are of the household of faith (Galatians 6:10). There will be times when the only positive interaction some people have is when they come to church. For others, you may have a particularly charismatic personality to which others gravitate. Your presence in church fuels those around you and is vital to the health of the entire body. Regardless of your participation in the local church, however, rest assured that the body of Christ will survive and thrive. But wouldn't you rather be where God wants to plant you instead of stuck in the belly of a fish (i.e., in a situation where you feel alone and isolated from others)? Remember, the enemy is roaming and in search of those who have separated themselves from the herd—or in this case, from the body. How can a plant grow if it does not have roots? Your connection to a local body grounds you and allows you to learn how to love and be good to one another.

Reason three: Being connected to a local church body means you are regularly hearing the voice of God. God uses songs, sermons, and Scriptures to communicate exactly what you need to hear. Remember, you serve a *God who sees you* and who understands what you need at any given time. You should enter your place of worship fully expecting to hear from God at each service and should fully participate in the entire service. Always expect to hear something that applies to your situation because God is expecting you to listen and follow him.

There may be some who believe listening to television ministry can supplant attendance in a local church. Television ministries have done a tremendous amount of work spreading the gospel throughout the world, and many people have received salvation based on a message they received via a televised ministry. I enjoy watching many of the ministers, including my own, on television. If, however, you limit yourself to only watching TV, you have limited your ability to make disciples of all nations. If you are physically able to regularly attend a church and have access to a local church body, you should really be in prayer about where God would have you attend.

God has designed you to receive spiritual instruction from a spiritual leader on a regular basis. In Proverbs, we learn that obtaining instruction and hearing counsel is necessary for wisdom later in life (Proverbs 19:20). Moreover, you are told to focus your attention on the instruction and to value the knowledge you receive (Proverbs 23:12).

Why should your spiritual leader instruct you? It demonstrates his or her love for God (John 21:15). The spiritual instruction you are to be fed by the pastor or minister (et al.) is God's Word. Your pastor receives the Word from God and plants the seed, the Word of God, in your heart by ministering to you. Your pastor has been designated to instruct God's people, and he or she is held accountable by God to do so (Isaiah 62:6 and Ezekiel 33:6).

"I have set watchmen upon thy walls, O Jerusalem, which shall never hold their peace day or night: ye that make mention of the Lord, keep not silence" (Isaiah 62:6–9, KJV). The pastor is not a substitute for your praying and seeking guidance from God. Nor is he or she to be your only contact with God. The blood of Jesus gives us confidence to enter into God's presence for ourselves (Hebrews 10:19). Instead, the pastor is the planter of the seed of the Word of God, because knowledge of God's divine will is not born within you. Revelation must be revealed to you (Matthew 28:20). The pastor speaks with boldness by the Holy Spirit to you in order to make known the mysteries of the gospel (Ephesians 6:19). The seeds are watered daily by meditation and prayer, and God causes the seeds to grow and produce fruit through your application of the Word in your own lives (I Corinthians 3:6). An intimate relationship with God is formed by spending time with God regularly and by praying about the instruction you were given through the pastor.

Is there a pastor who can speak into your life and offer you instruction? Having a church home does not necessarily mean you are receiving the instruction you need from God. There may be many churches throughout your community that have quality messages from God being ministered. Does this mean you can be a member of all these local bodies? Certainly not! God has called each one of you to receive your instruction at one particular church submitted to a pastor (Ezekiel 34:23).

If you are receiving quality instruction and you are where God has called you to be, you should appreciate and respect the pastor at that church and receive the instruction coming through him or her from the Holy Spirit. You should also be regularly praying for him or her that he might open his mouth boldly to make known the mystery of the gospel (Ephesians 6:19). Although we will look at this principle in detail later in following chapters, now is the perfect opportunity to thank God for the man of God he has given you.

The Second Scroll

Seven Tips for Effective Personal Prayer Life

First Tip: Begin Your Prayer with Worship

Second Tip: Conduct an Examination of Your Attitudes and Actions

Third Tip: Pray with the Word of God

Fourth Tip: Pray Continually

Fifth Tip: Take Time to Listen to the Father

Sixth Tip: Establish Prayer Partners

Seventh Tip: Connect with a Local Church Body

Pray for Others

Creed III

We believe that because God loves the world, it is our responsibility to pray for it.

Chapter 10

No Excuses

When was the last time you prayed for someone who is not a family member or close friend? I excluded family and close friends because oftentimes those prayers directly impact you or your own situation. I am talking about praying for people from whom you may never receive thanks or benefits.

Andrew, my youngest, likes praying for others. Like many children, he has a pretty active imagination. When you couple the desire to pray with others with a creative imagination, the result is ten minutes of prayers for his friends at school, neighbors, his teacher, and even his brother. He frequently prays that his brother would allow him to play with his game system. On the surface, I am proud that he is praying for his brother, but when you dig a little deeper, you realize his prayer is out of selfishness. At six, he has good intentions, and his father and I will continue to train him as he has the makings of a true prayer warrior. When you think about praying for others, you want to make sure you are not doing so out of selfish reasons.

In these next few chapters, we will focus on praying for those with whom you are in a relationship and those with whom you have no direct contact. Why is this important?

Praying for others is directly connected to your own blessings and personal breakthroughs. Consider Job, as mentioned earlier. Job lost everything! After he prayed for his friends, as God instructed, he received an even greater blessing (Job 42:10). In fact, the Lord restored his fortunes and gave him twice as much as he had before.

We cannot use the excuse that we are facing our own problems and therefore are not in a position to pray for others. This is a selfish attitude. Paul was imprisoned when he wrote to the Philippians. He was physically and mentally exhausted. He was in a terrible condition. He may have been living in a cave or dungeon when he wrote to them. Read this excerpt from his letter to the Philippians and decide if it reads as if he were in dire conditions and concerned with alleviating his own suffering.

> And this I pray: that your love may abound yet more and more and extend to its fullest development in knowledge and all keen insight that your love may display itself in greater depth of acquaintance and more comprehensive discernment, so that you may surely learn to sense what is vital, and approve and prize what is excellent and of real value recognizing the highest and the best, and distinguishing the moral differences, and that you may be untainted and pure and unerring and blameless so that with hearts sincere and certain and unsullied, you may approach the day of Christ not stumbling nor causing others to stumble. May you abound in and be filled with the fruits of righteousness (of right standing with God and right doing) which come through Jesus Christ (the Anointed One), to the honor and praise of God that His glory may be both manifested and recognized. Now I want you to know and continue to rest assured, brethren, that what has happened to me

this imprisonment has actually only served to advance and give a renewed impetus to the spreading of the good news (the gospel). (Philippians 1:9–12, AMP)

Paul is praying about love, excellent prizes, blameless hearts, and praising God. Not what you would expect from someone imprisoned in a cave. Regardless of the challenges that we face, this does not give us the excuse not to pray for one another. Paul cautions us not to become weary or discouraged when we are doing good. Galatians 6:9 reads: "Let us not become weary in doing good, for at the proper time we will reap a harvest if we do not give up". So do we only pray for others when we are in the midst of a trial?

Even if you are not experiencing challenges or have no difficulty in your life, the Word of God is clear about our expectation that we pray for one another. In his letter to the Ephesians, Paul writes that we should be alert and consistently praying for God's people. Thus, we should not just wait for someone to ask us to pray for him or her but are to look for opportunities to pray for others (Ephesians 6:18). Timothy instructs us to make petitions, intercessions, and thanksgiving for all people (I Timothy 2:1–6, 8). Not only should we be alert and ready to pray for others, we should use all kinds of prayers and requests. In Hebrews, we see the author describing creative imaginings or thoughts about his friends and their salvation (Hebrews 6:9).

Do you have a friend who is not saved? What would he or she be like if this person were saved? How would this impact your relationship? Pray for him or her to receive salvation.

Consider Esther, who asked people pray and fast for her when she was going to approach the king: "Then Esther told them to give this answer to Mordecai, go, gather together all the Jews that are present in Shushan, and fast for me; and neither eat nor drink for three days, night or day. I also and my maids will fast as you do. Then I will go to the king, though it is against the law; and if I perish, I perish" (Esther

4:15–16, AMP). What Esther was trying to do was too heavy for her to accomplish alone. Paul writes in Galatians that we should carry one another's burdens (Galatians 6:2). There are some situations that require support from others. Who is there to help the man who falls alone? Thus we should display a "we are in this together" attitude.

Having a Compassionate Heart

I am a firm believer that some people, even in the face of our selfish human nature, are able to have a compassionate heart without much effort. My husband is one of these people. When I was teaching at a high school in Memphis, I brought home a student who needed a temporary place to stay. My husband was the one who insisted we do all that we could to support her. Fast forward thirteen years, and Tanzye has been with us ever since. She has been more of a blessing to us than we were to her. Our house is her home, and it is because of my husband's desire to alleviate her distress and his efforts to follow this desire with action.

According to the *Merriam-Webster* dictionary, compassion is defined as "sympathetic consciousness of others' distress together with a desire to alleviate it." We must have a heart for others as demonstrated by our commitment to pray for our community, our nation, and our world. Our desire to want to alleviate others' distress, our prayers, and our acts of faith will help us fulfill our goal as members of the body, which is to make disciples.

As an educator, I remember one of the first things my first school principal shared with me. He told me the students will not care what you know unless they know you care. I have heard that saying countless times and have even used it when conducting workshops on classroom management. That same principle can be applied here. Some people do not want to know *your* Jesus until they know that *your* Jesus cares for them. The "fire and brimstone" method has always carried a certain appeal for some as they preach about salvation. The majority of people in our world just need to know there is a savior who loves them and cares about them.

My pastor, John Seibling, oftentimes shares with us statistics about poverty across the globe, and I am always amazed at how many children go to bed hungry at night. Part of our mission as members of the body of Christ is to pray for those children, not just our own. As James writes, when we pray with selfish motives, our prayers are hindered (James 4:3). The author goes on to remind us that we are to pray for each other so we can be healed (James 5:16). According to the Amplified Bible, this idea of being healed refers to being restored to a spiritual tone of mind and heart. As mentioned earlier, our own spiritual health and well-being is directly related to our commitment to pray for one another. If you would not like your prayers to be hindered and you desire to have a healthy physical and spiritual life, you must commit to praying for one another.

So what do we pray for others? We are going to do a thirty-day challenge. We will add sixty seconds to our prayer time once a day to pray for someone else. We will pray for our government leaders, our children, the city we live in, and more! Make these prayers part of your prayer arsenal and watch how God will use you to bless those around you. Make prayer cards, and use them to help you. You have prayer "stems" on the following pages that you may use verbatim, or you may add to them or modify them by substituting names. A prayer stem is simply a phrase to start your prayers. Your selfless acts will not be in vain. If you skip a day, jump back in! If it's the sixteenth day of the month, for example, pray day sixteen. Start wherever you are.

Imagine how many prayers we could bombard heaven with if we all joined in and prayed for others every day. As you continue to be faithful in praying for others, you will become more compassionate. You will be supporting your desire to help others alleviate their distress through prayer. In addition, as you pray for others, know that

God has not forgotten about your concerns or needs. Your selflessness will be a catalyst to your own answered prayer.

Let's begin!

Chapter 11

Pray for Children

Day 1 Pray for the children to be taught about God.

"Teach them to your children and to their children after them" (Deuteronomy 4:9–10).

Father God, I pray that our children would be taught from an early age about you. I declare they will develop an appetite for godly things and hunger and thirst for you.

Day 2 Pray for children to receive salvation.

"Jesus said, 'Let the little children come to me, and do not hinder them, for the kingdom of heaven belongs to such as these'" (Matthew 19:14).

Father, our healer, I pray over our children that they would hasten to your throne of glory without shrinking back or in opposition. I pray that your Word and your power alone would have free course in their lives.

Day 3 Pray for children to have a relationship with God.

"When the religious leaders saw the outrageous things he was doing and heard all the children running and shouting through the temple, 'Hosanna to David's Son!' they were up in arms and took him to task. 'Do you hear what these children are saying?' Jesus said, 'Yes, I hear them. And haven't you read in God's Word, "From the mouths of children and babies I'll furnish a place of praise"?'" (Matthew 21:15, MSG).

God of glory, I pray our children would shout praises unto you because you alone are worthy. I pray their mouths would be filled with words of praise and thanksgiving.

Day 4 Pray for the way children are taught and the people teaching them.

"Fathers, do not irritate and provoke your children to anger [do not exasperate them to resentment], but rear them [tenderly] in the training and discipline and the counsel and admonition of the Lord" (Ephesians 6:4, AMP).

God of knowledge, I declare that those who are in authority over our children would teach them according to the principles found in your Word. I pray that they would lead them gently as they teach them about you.

Day 5 Pray for children to be obedient.

"Children, obey your parents in everything, for this is pleasing to the Lord" (Colossians 3:20, AMP).

Righteous God, I proclaim that our children would do what their parents or guardians tell them to do. Father, give them an obedient and humble spirit.

Day 6 Pray for children to have the right kind of friends who help them make good choices.

"My son, if sinners entice you, do not consent. If they say, Come with us; let us lie in wait to shed blood, let us ambush the innocent without cause and show that his piety is in vain" (Proverbs 1:10–11, AMP).

You are an everlasting God. Lord, I pray that our children would be surrounded by godly influences. I pray that young men and women of God would always give them counsel as they ignore those who are ungodly and follow the ways of sin.

Chapter 12

Pray for Women

Day 7 Pray that she would trust in the Lord.

"Lean on, trust in, and be confident in the Lord with all your heart and mind and do not rely on your own insight or understanding. In all your ways know, recognize, and acknowledge him, and he will direct and make straight and plain your paths" (Proverbs 3:5–6, AMP).

Thank you, Father, for being faithful in the lives of women everywhere. I pray they will honor you and not try to figure things out on their own. They will be women who listen for your voice in everything they do and everywhere they go.

Day 8 Pray that she would be humble, gentle, and patient.

"Living as becomes you with complete lowliness of mind (humility) and meekness (unselfishness, gentleness, mildness), with patience, bearing with one another and making allowances because you love one another" (Ephesians 4:2, AMP).

Almighty God, I pray you would raise up women who are unselfish, gentle, humble, and patient. I thank you for women in this world who are loving to those with whom they come in contact.

Day 9 Pray that she will be devoted to the Lord.

I would like you to be free from concern. An unmarried man is concerned about the Lord's affairs—how he can please the Lord. But a married man is concerned about the affairs of this world—how he can please his wife—and his interests are divided. An unmarried woman or virgin is concerned about the Lord's affairs: Her aim is to be devoted to the Lord in both body and spirit. But a married woman is concerned about the affairs of this world—how she can please her husband. I am saying this for your own good, not to restrict you, but that you may live in a right way in undivided devotion to the Lord. (1 Corinthians 7:32–35)

You are a God who sees us and knows us. I declare that unmarried women would be concerned with pleasing you and not men. I also declare that married women across the world would love their husbands and be devoted to them out of love and devotion to you.

Day 10 Pray that her mannerisms would worship God.

"I also want the women to dress modestly, with decency and propriety, adorning themselves, not with elaborate hairstyles or gold or pearls or expensive clothes, but with good deeds, appropriate for women who profess to worship God" (1 Timothy 2:9–10).

Heavenly Father, I pray that women of God would carry themselves in a way befitting the calling. I proclaim their actions, conversations, and attitudes would worship you.

Day 11 Pray that she would have wisdom and know how to respond in every situation.

"Let your conversation be always full of grace, seasoned with salt, so that you may know how to answer everyone" (Colossians 4:6).

Father God, I pray that their conversations would be full of grace and that they would have wisdom and know how to respond to everyone in every situation.

Chapter 13

Pray for Men

Day 12 Pray that he would love his wife as Christ loves the church.

"Husbands, love your wives, just as Christ loved the church and gave himself up for her to make her holy, cleansing her by the washing with water through the word, and to present her to himself as a radiant church, without stain or wrinkle or any other blemish, but holy and blameless. In this same way, husbands ought to love their wives as their own bodies. He who loves his wife loves himself" (Ephesians 5:25–28).

You, o Lord, are the Lord of my life. I pray that you would raise up godly men who love their wives with an attitude of giving and not of getting. I pray that husbands would love their wives as Christ loves his church.

Day 13 Pray for his wisdom when teaching his children.

"Fathers, do not embitter your children, or they will become discouraged" (Colossians 3:21).

God of compassion, I pray that our fathers/guardians would not come down too hard on their children, thereby crushing their spirit. I pray their words would bring life and encouragement to their children.

Day 14 Pray for him to have godly goals.

"Though I myself have reasons for such confidence. If someone else thinks they have reasons to put confidence in the flesh, I have more: Brothers and sisters, I do not consider myself yet to have taken hold of it. But one thing I do: Forgetting what is behind and straining toward what is ahead, I press on toward the goal to win the prize for which God has called me heavenward in Christ Jesus" (Philippians 3:4,13–14).

Awesome God, I pray that our men would have godly goals and would not turn back from you but would run to you focused on achieving all that you have established.

Day 15 Pray that he would be an example to younger men.

"Teach the older men to be temperate, worthy of respect, self-controlled, and sound in faith, in love and in endurance. Similarly, encourage the young men to be self-controlled. In everything set them an example by doing what is good. In your teaching show integrity, seriousness and soundness of speech that cannot be condemned, so that those who oppose you may be ashamed because they have nothing bad to say about us" (Titus 2:2, 6–8).

God of my strength, I declare our men would be an example to younger men by living a life of temperance, dignity, wisdom, love, and endurance.

Day 16 Pray for them to be leaders who follow.

"Not so with you. Instead, whoever wants to become great among you must be your servant, and whoever wants to be first must be slave of all. For even the Son of Man did not come to be served but to serve" (Mark 10:43–45).

Holy God, I proclaim that our men are committed to following you and reverently fear you. They are men who serve their families, communities, and churches as Christ served others.

Chapter 14

Pray for Neighbors

Day 17 Pray that they would hunger and thirst for God.

"Create in me a pure heart, O God, and renew a steadfast spirit within me. Do not cast me from your presence or take your Holy Spirit from me. Restore to me the joy of my salvation and grant me a willing spirit, to sustain me" (Psalm 51:10–12).

"He humbled you, causing you to hunger and then feeding you with manna, which neither you nor your ancestors had known, to teach you that man does not live on bread alone but on every word that comes from the mouth of the Lord" (Deuteronomy 8:3).

"Blessed are those who hunger and thirst for righteousness, for they will be filled" (Matthew 5:6).

God of the heavens, I pray that our neighbors would want to know more about you- and that you would cause them to hunger and thirst for you.

Day 18 Pray that they would be knowledgeable of their purpose.

"May the God of hope fill you with all joy and peace as you trust in him, so that you may overflow with hope by the power of the Holy Spirit" (Romans 15:13).

"Many are the plans in a person's heart, but it is the Lord's purpose that prevails" (Proverbs 19:21).

God, fill our neighbors with joy and peace as they trust in you with their whole heart. Allow them to know their purpose and overflow with the anointing of your Holy Spirit.

Day 19 Pray that they would love God.

"Jesus replied: 'Love the Lord your God with all your heart and with all your soul and with all your mind. This is the first and greatest commandment. And the second is like it: Love your neighbor as yourself. All the law and the prophets hang on these two commandments'" (Matthew 22:37–40).

Merciful God, I thank you for neighbors who love you with their inmost being. I ask that their whole hearts be filled, saturated, and covered in your love.

Day 20 Pray for the oppressed in the world.

"The Lord reigns forever; he has established his throne for judgment. He rules the world in righteousness and judges the peoples with equity. The Lord is a refuge for the oppressed, a stronghold in times of trouble" (Psalm 9:7–9).

God of compassion, you are sovereign and reign forever. I ask you to be a safe hiding place for those in trouble across this world. I pray that you would lift up the oppressed and judge with equity.

Chapter 15

Pray for the City or Town

Day 21 Pray that your city/town would have peace and be safe.

"I urge, then, first of all, that petitions, prayers, intercession and thanksgiving be made for all people—for kings and all those in authority, that we may live peaceful and quiet lives in all godliness and holiness. This is good, and pleases God our Savior, who wants all people to be saved and to come to the knowledge of truth" (1 Timothy 2:1–4).

God of peace, I declare that our neighbors have peace in their souls and are safe wherever they go. I also declare that they are godly and holy members of our community.

Day 22 Pray for it to be a righteous and faithful city.

"I will restore your leaders as in days of old, your rulers as at the beginning. Afterward you will be called the city of righteousness, the faithful city" (Isaiah 1:26).

Righteous God, I ask for you to set honest and wise leaders over us, and I declare our city will be known as a city that treats people right.

Day 23 Pray for your city to be prosperous.

"Also, seek the peace and prosperity of the city to which I have carried you into exile. Pray to the Lord for it, because if it prospers, you too will prosper" (Jeremiah 29:7).

Heavenly Father, I pray for people in our city/country to work together for the welfare of our city/country. I ask that things go well in our city/state and believe that as they go well with our city/state, they would go well for us.

Chapter 16

Pray for the Leaders in the City, State, and National Government

Day 24 Pray that they would be leaders who are full of wisdom and the Holy Spirit.

"Brothers and sisters, choose seven men from among you who are known to be full of the Spirit and wisdom. We will turn this responsibility over to them and will give our attention to prayer and the ministry of the word" (Acts 6:3–4).

God, I pray the leaders of our local, state, and national governments would be godly leaders who receive their wisdom from you. I declare this is the truth for our mayors, governors, presidents, and others in leadership positions in our world.

Day 25 Pray that they would be good, trustworthy leaders.

"But select capable men from all the people—men who fear God, trustworthy men who hate dishonest gain—and appoint them as officials over thousands, hundreds, fifties, and tens" (Exodus 18:21).

God of my strength, I pray for the leaders in our world to be competent, God-fearing men of integrity who are incorruptible. I ask that they would establish leaders who are responsible for and responsive to your people.

Day 26 Pray that we would be sensitive to multiculturalism and tolerant of one another.

"For the Lord your God is God of gods and Lord of lords, the great God, mighty and awesome, who shows no partiality and accepts no bribes. He defends the cause of the fatherless and the widow, and loves the foreigner residing among you, giving them food and clothing. And you are to love those who are foreigners, for you yourselves were foreigners in Egypt" (Deuteronomy 10:17–19).

Mighty and awesome God, you defend those who cannot defend themselves. Just as you love all of your children regardless of where they were born, I pray that we would love them, too.

Chapter 17

Pray for the Unsaved

Day 27 Pray that they would seek God.

"If my people, who are called by my name, will humble themselves and pray and seek my face and turn from their wicked ways, then I will hear from heaven, and I will forgive their sin and will heal their land" (2 Chronicles 7:14).

Merciful God, our healer, I declare that your people are humble and repentant. I pray that as they continue to pray and seek your face that you would forgive them and heal both them and their land.

Day 28 Pray that God's children would be obedient to him.

"So that you, your children and their children after them may fear the Lord your God as long as you live by keeping all his decrees and commands that I give you, and so that you may enjoy long life" (Deuteronomy 6:2).

Heavenly Father, I proclaim that we, as your children, are obedient to your Word and reverently fear you as our Lord. As we do this, Lord, I pray that we would enjoy a long, peaceful, and prosperous life.

Day 29 Pray for the unsaved to receive salvation.

"For God so loved the world that he gave his one and only Son, that whoever believes in him shall not perish but have eternal life" (John 3:16).

God our redeemer, I declare you are a God of love who gave his best to us. I pray that those who have not come into the knowledge of truth would accept you as their personal savior. I ask that you would continue to equip me to be a witness to them of your love and kindness. Use me, Lord!

Day 30 Pray for whatever you desire to pray. Be sure to use a scriptural reference.

Scripture

_____

_____

_____

_____

_____

Prayer

_____

_____

_____

_____

_____

Is prayer enough? No—we must back our faith with our actions (James 2:18). We are justified before God when our actions support our faith (James 2:24). Everyone has a responsibility to sow his or her talent or time to help someone who is in need. It is our responsibility, and it demonstrates our obedience and love of God. If you love God, prove it—love your neighbor and pray for him or her!

The Third Scroll

Praying for others is directly connected to your own blessings and personal breakthroughs.

Regardless of the challenges that we face, this does not give us the excuse not to pray for one another.

We should display a "we are in this together" attitude.

We must have a heart for others as demonstrated by our commitment to pray for our community, our nation, and our world.

For some people, they do not want to know *your* Jesus, until they know that *your* Jesus cares for them.

As you pray for others, know that God has not forgotten about your concerns or needs.

Seven Prayers for a Highly Effective Local Body

Creed IV

We believe we have a special responsibility to pray for our local church as it fulfills the great commission in this world.

Chapter 18

Parts Represent the Whole

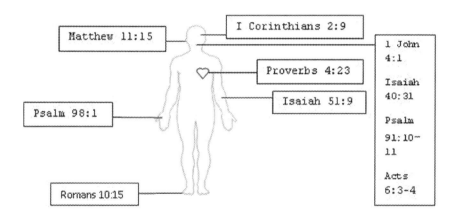

The body of Christ represents the group of people all across our world that are believers. For our discussion here, the body of Christ represents both the church as a whole, and as a distinct, organized local entity. In this chapter, we will focus on our responsibility to pray for our local church as it fulfills the Great Commission. Because the part, which is the local church, cannot exist in isolation of the whole, you should develop a prayer life whereby you pray for both.

Consider what Paul writes about the body of Christ:

Just as a body, though one, has many parts, but all its many parts form one body, so it is with Christ. For we were all baptized by one Spirit so as to form one body—whether Jews or Gentiles, slave or free—and we were all given the one Spirit to drink. Even so the body is not made up of one part but of many. Now if the foot should say, "Because I am not a hand, I do not belong to the body," it would not for that reason stop being part of the body. And if the ear should say, "Because I am not an eye, I do not belong to the body," it would not for that reason stop being part of the body. If the whole body were an eye, where would the sense of hearing be? If the whole body were an ear, where would the sense of smell be? But in fact God has placed the parts in the body, every one of them, just as he wanted them to be. If they were all one part, where would the body be? As it is, there are many parts, but one body. (1 Corinthians 12:12–20)

Christ is the head of the body (Romans 12:5), and the members of the body of Christ represent the people whom God has called to be members of the church. Each part of our natural body, like the body of Christ, has a distinct function. Our eyes enable us to see, and our hands allow us to accomplish specific tasks. Just as the body can be used as a metaphor for the group of believers, it can also be used to show us how to pray for the attributes the local body should have.

There are seven parts of your natural body that I want us to explore in order to learn how to pray for the body of Christ. These parts represent different principles that make up the diversity of the functions of the body of Christ. As you read and meditate on the Scriptures, use the names of God listed earlier in your book to develop your own prayers for your local church.

Chapter 19

Prayer 1: The Feet

And how can anyone preach unless they are sent? As it is written: How beautiful are the feet of those who bring good news!

—Romans 10:15

The feet are essential elements in our ability to physically move. They represent the church's role in sharing the gospel throughout the nation and making disciples of others and baptizing them in the name of the Father, the Son, and the Holy Spirit (Matthew 28). This is the Great Commission. In the local church, each member should concern himself and herself with actively supporting the Great Commission. When you walk, one foot is always moving while the other foot supports the weight of the entire body.

You should pray the local church would do two main things. First pray there are workers who actively move about the community sharing the good news with others. Isaiah tells us that the feet enable the body to bring good news, proclaim peace, and circulate information about salvation (Isaiah 52:7). Next you should pray for members who support this work through spiritual and financial contributions. Without the continual prayers for this work and the financial contributions that enable the work to be done, the body of Christ would not be fulfilling its role in spreading the gospel.

Prayer: _____

_____

_____

_____

_____

_____

_____

_____

_____

Chapter 20

Prayer 2: The Arms

Awake, awake, arm of the Lord, clothe yourself with
strength! Awake, as in days gone by, as in generations
of old.

—Isaiah 51:9

Your arms enable you to reach for objects that are not connected to it.
The strength and power needed to reach for objects with your hands
are accomplished with your arms. The arm of the Lord represents the
extension of God's power. God asks Moses if his arm was too short
to perform miracles (Numbers 11:23). God's power was manifested
when he created us in his image. God's power is limitless, and the
arms of the church represent this limitless power. Your prayer for your
local church should be that God's power would be unleashed through
the members of the body in order to accomplish his purpose.

Lischa T. Brooks

Prayer: _____

_____

_____

_____

_____

_____

_____

_____

_____

_____

Chapter 21

Prayer 3: The Hands

Sing to the Lord a new song, for he has done marvelous things; his right hand and his holy arm have worked salvation for him.

—Psalm 98:1

Your hands are an extension of your arms. Among many uses, you use your hands are used to touch. The hands also represent "doing" something (Ecclesiastes 9:10). When you hear the idiom "my hands are tied," it means someone is restrained from doing something. Also, the hands bring reward (Proverbs 12:14). Your prayer for the local body should be that every ministry would be effective, efficient, and equipped to work together. Pray for the *tasks* of each ministry to be successful, the *talents* of each member to be shared, and the *tithe,* which makes it possible to *touch* the community to be given.

Lischa T. Brooks

Prayer: _____
_____
_____
_____
_____
_____
_____
_____
_____
_____

Chapter 22

Prayer 4: The Heart

Above all else, guard your heart, for everything you
do flows from it.

—Proverbs 4:23

Your heart plays the most important role in circulation. The heart
enables oxygen-rich blood to flow throughout the body to nourish
every system, organ, and cell. So significant is the heart that it
starts to pump when you are a few weeks old in utero. The heart
is used throughout the Bible to represent the "inner man." The
heart represents the emotion, will, and thoughts of man. For this
reason, you should pray for the local church to be the center of
enlightenment, encouragement, and exhortation of the members.
The local body should be the main source of *enlightenment* for the
members as they increase in knowledge of God and their relationship
with him. You should pray that the members receive *encouragement*
from being connected with a local body. Finally, you should pray that
members receive *exhortation* or instruction from their local body on
how to apply the Word to their lives.

Prayer:

_____

_____

_____

_____

_____

_____

_____

_____

_____

_____

Chapter 23

Prayer 5: The Eyes

However, as it is written: "What no eye has seen, what no ear has heard, and what no human mind has conceived"—the things God has prepared for those who love him."

—1 Corinthians 2:9

Your eyes enable you to see. The eyes of the local body represent vision. Pray for the vision of the church as shared by the pastor of the church. Without a vision, the members of the body and the local body itself would decay (Proverbs 29:18). Therefore, the vision of the church is essential for the health and well-being of each member. Pray that the pastor of your local church would receive revelation from God about the vision of the church, and that he or she would be able to communicate that vision to the members. Also pray that the pastor would be able to see clearly the wonderful things in the Word of God (Psalm 119:18).

Lischa T. Brooks

Prayer: _____
_____
_____
_____
_____
_____
_____
_____
_____
_____

Chapter 24

Prayer 6: The Ears

Whoever has ears, let them hear.

—Matthew 11:15

Seeing and hearing often work collaboratively to strengthen our understanding of something. You should pray that your local church body would be led by a pastor who hears clearly from God. You should also pray that your fellow members would hear what was being shared as the Word of God. The members of the local body have to be willing to hear the Word and then pray for understanding of the application of that Word in their lives.

Lischa T. Brooks

Prayer: _____

_____

_____

_____

_____

_____

_____

_____

_____

_____

Chapter 25

Prayer 7: The Mouth

Jesus answered, "It is written: 'Man does not live on bread alone, but on every word that comes from the mouth of God.'"

—Matthew 4:4

The mouth of God represents the pastor and leadership team that have been charged with speaking what God has instructed. There are four main areas you should pray for your pastor and leadership team.

To Have a Discerning Spirit

"Dear friends, do not believe every spirit, but test the spirits to see whether they are from God, because many false prophets have gone out into the world" (1 John 4:1).

Father, I pray my pastor would have a discerning spirit and the wisdom to know how to recognize your voice and how to apply your Word for our local body.

To Continue to Receive Rest and Renewal

"but those who hope in the Lord will renew their strength. They will soar on wings like eagles; they will run and not grow weary; they will walk and not be faint" (Isaiah 40:31).

God, you are my rock and my strength. I pray that you would continue to strengthen the man of God that you have given to our local church. I pray that you would renew his or her strength and empower every person to accomplish your work here on earth.

To Have Protection for Their Family

"no harm will overtake you, no disaster will come near your tent. For he will command his angels concerning you to guard you in all your ways" (Psalm 91:10–11).

Omnipotent God, I declare that all power is in your hands. I pray you would protect our pastor and his or her family and that no harm, disaster, evil plan, or attack will harm them. I thank you, Father, for giving your angels charge over protecting them and keeping them safe.

To Be Spirit-Led and Wise Leaders

"Brothers and sisters, choose seven men from among you who are known to be full of the Spirit and wisdom. We will turn this responsibility over to them and will give our attention to prayer and the ministry of the word" (Acts 6:3–4).

Father, you are the architect of wisdom. All wisdom comes from you. I pray the pastor would operate in your wisdom. I pray he or she would receive counsel from you and would be led by your Holy Spirit. Father, I thank you for selecting our pastor, and I will be careful to honor the gift you have given us in our pastor.

Prayer: _____

_____

_____

_____

_____

_____

_____

_____

_____

_____

Chapter 26

The Prayer Ministry

The purpose of the prayer ministry is to actively encourage and promote prayer within the life of the church. The prayer ministry consists of church leaders, members, or community members. Prayer-team members must have an attitude of compassion toward people.

Consider this Scripture for the establishment of a prayer ministry: "This is the confidence we have in approaching God: that if we ask anything according to his will, he hears us. And if we know that he hears us—whatever we ask—we know that we have what we asked of him" (1 John 5:14–15).

The focus of the prayer ministry cannot simply be physical healings or issues. While you do want to pray for physical needs, this cannot become the primary focus of the prayer ministry. The pastor or other church leader may give you specific prayer requests. Just like you begin your personal prayer time with worship, the prayer ministry should begin with a period of praise and thanksgiving. When you pray out of an attitude of worship, the focus is more God-centered and less needs-centered or emotion-centered.

Participation on a prayer team may occur one or two ways. One church may decide each member of the team should be selected by the leadership team. While at another church, there may be a more open membership process. Regardless of how the team is established, all members should have a desire to pray with people. It is imperative that each member is open and responsive to the Holy Spirit in prayer. When necessary, the church leaders may provide training. In most instances, people coming for prayer or providing written prayer requests can expect strict confidentiality. If something that concerns the prayer team is shared by a member, they must discuss it with the church leadership so they can decide the next steps in that situation.

Prayer Team Focus

In general, there are four main areas that should be a priority for the prayer team. First, you should pray for your specific community and needs within your community. Second, you should pray for the church and any ministry or program in the church. Next, the prayer team should pray for physical, emotional, financial, and interpersonal healings and deliverance. Finally, the prayer ministry must pray for the local church leaders and their families. You should pray for their spiritual, physical, and mental well-being.

In addition, there may be times the church leaders will require the prayer team to pray for specific events or upcoming church activities. For example, a church could announce that on a certain night, members should meet to pray about the missions program of the church. The prayer team might meet in advance with the missions team or church leaders to pray and plan a service to engage in serious prayer for the missionaries.

There are many opportunities for the prayer team, and some churches take a systematic approach to their prayer ministry. As a church, you should encourage people to feel free to come for prayer for themselves and for others they are concerned about.

Thinking Inside the Box

The prayer team should meet weekly to focus on the church service, in general. As a member of a prayer team, you should expect the Spirit to guide your prayers, perhaps with words of wisdom, knowledge, or comfort. For the pre-service prayer, *think inside the box.* Let's examine four main areas around which a pre-service prayer team may elect to focus.

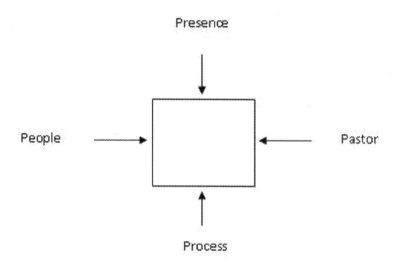

The box contains the four Ps for pre-service prayer team assembly: pray for the **p**resence of the Holy Spirit, your **p**astor and other church leaders, the **p**eople of God, and the **p**rocess that occurs during the actual service. While the prayer team may not have a need to pray for all four areas each time you assemble, you want to be sure to frame your prayer focus around these areas as appropriate. The church leaders may provide a specific agenda or focus for each meeting.

The Presence

When you pray for the presence of the Holy Spirit, remember what Matthew tells us happens when people gather together in the name of God: "For where two or three gather in my name, there am I with them" (Matthew 18:20). This means you should pray for the attendees to assemble expecting for God's Holy Spirit to meet them at church. You should also pray for the Holy Spirit to guide the flow of the service.

The Pastor

Next you should pray for your pastor and other leaders in your church. You should pray God will equip them with everything good for doing his will (Hebrews 13:21). Your prayer team should always pray the pastors would be equipped and ready to minister to God's people. In addition, you should pray they will not become weary while they are doing good (Galatians 6:9).

The People

Intercessory prayer is primarily focused on making requests on behalf of others. You may not initially know how to pray for this need, but you as you begin to pray you sense the Holy Spirit guiding your prayers (Romans 8:26–27). This guidance may be in the form of prayer in your native language, or in your supernatural language, (i.e., praying in tongues). The prayer team is not to be used for counseling. If someone needs counseling, he or she may wish to make arrangements to discuss a particular need or concern with the leadership.

When you pray for God's people, you are praying for four main areas: freedom, deliverance, healing, and salvation.

God's Word gives us freedom and this freedom leads to blessings. James writes, "Anyone who listens to the word but does not do what it says is like a man who looks at his face in a mirror and, after looking at himself, goes away and immediately forgets what he looks like. But the man who looks intently into the perfect law that gives freedom, and continues to do this, not forgetting what he has heard, but doing it—he will be blessed in what he does" (James 1:23–25).

Freedom leads to success and peace. Consider these Scriptures:

"Save us, we pray, O LORD! O LORD, we pray, give us success!" (Psalm 118:25).

"Pray for the peace of Jerusalem! May they be secure who love you!" (Psalm 122:6).

Therefore, when you pray for the freedom of God's people, you are praying that God's people would have peaceful and victorious lives as a result of the Word they receive from the service. Also, you are praying that they would be free to hear the Word of God and obey.

Next you should pray for deliverance. God's people will face trials—there will come a day of trouble. "Offer to God a sacrifice of thanksgiving, and perform your vows to the Most High, and call upon me in the day of trouble; I will deliver you, and you shall glorify me" (Psalm 50:14–15). You should have confidence in God's sovereignty and know you will not face the day of trouble alone. You should always pray for those who may be in attendance who need deliverance from situations. Whether they face financial, spiritual, or physical challenges, God knows and is able to deliver them into a better place.

Next you should pray for those people who attend service—or those who may not be in attendance—who need to receive salvation. As believers, we have accepted salvation, but it is our responsibility to lead others to Christ and to pray for them while they are being led. Paul writes in Romans that his heart's desire and prayer is that these individuals would be saved (Romans 10:1).

Finally you should pray for any healing that needs to manifest among the members. "Therefore, confess your sins to one another and pray for one another, that you may be healed. The prayer of a righteous person has great power as it is working" (James 5:16).

The Process

In addition to praying for the presence of the Holy Spirit to manifest and for the pastors and other church leaders and the people of God, your final charge is to pray for the actual church service: the process. Praying for the process means praying for an atmosphere of true worship, believers who would hear the Word and do what it demands, and for unity among the body of the church. It means praying for everyone to be fully engaged and ready to hear from God. The mantra for unity in the body of Christ could be found in Ephesians 4:29–32: "Let no corrupting talk come out of your mouths, but only such as is good for building up, as fits the occasion, that it may give grace to those who hear. And do not grieve the Holy Spirit of God, by whom you were sealed for the day of redemption. Let all bitterness and wrath and anger and clamor and slander be put away from you, along with all malice. Be kind to one another, tenderhearted, forgiving one another, as God in Christ forgave you."

Following the service, the prayer team might pray with specific people. Perhaps an attendee has asked for prayer or someone on the team may be led to pray with a church attendee. Prayer with people after the service should normally be done in twos and should be gender sensitive.

How do you pray for someone? If you do not know the person you are praying with, start by introducing yourself, and ask for a brief outline of the prayer need. If appropriate, you may offer him or her the opportunity to join in the prayer. Be sure to thank the person for taking a step of faith and asking for prayer. If appropriate, you may get his or her contact information so you can contact that person later in the week.

A healthy personal prayer life leads to a more effective and enthusiastic corporate prayer experience. We all have a responsibility to pray for our local church. Moreover, those who have an additional purpose to pray for the church should commit themselves to going even deeper in prayer.

The Fourth Scroll

It is on our responsibility to pray for our local church as it fulfills the Great Commission.

Just as the body can be used as a metaphor for the group of believers, it can also be used to show us how to pray for the attributes that the local body should have.

Think inside the box. Pray for the presence of the Holy Spirit, your pastor and other church leaders, the people of God, and the process that occurs during the actual service.

You should also pray for the Holy Spirit to guide the flow of the service.

You should pray that God would equip them with everything good for doing His will (Hebrews 13:21).

When you pray for God's people, you are praying for four main areas: freedom, deliverance, healing, and salvation.

Praying for the process means praying for there to be an atmosphere of true worship, believers who would hear the word and do what it demands, and for unity among the body of the church.

Seven Steps toward Unleashing Supernatural Strength in Difficult Situations

Creed V

We believe an effective personal prayer life coupled with our willingness to pray for others unleashes the supernatural power within us when we are faced with challenges and opposition.

Chapter 27

The Attitude Arsenal

There may be seasons in your life when you may feel as if a never-ending barrage of attacks, struggles, and constant challenges have been strung together to create that season. Challenges will come, but you should have seasons of stasis in your life when you can breathe. As you continue to tap into your supernatural strength, you will even experience seasons of spiritual prosperity and peace. If you find you experience only constant struggles and challenges, continue to attend church and apply the Word to your life. You read earlier about the necessity to have a pastor who can speak over you and your life. You must be in a place where you can get a constant diet of the Word so you can grow up in your salvation (1 Peter 2:2–3).

Additionally, if you only see the negative in every situation, your perceptions may need readjusting. Maybe you need to look at your life differently. Are you only focusing on the negative and going through each day expecting challenges? If this is the case, learn how to renew your mind and look for opportunities to celebrate the good that happens.

If you woke up this morning, that means your life still has purpose and meaning. It means God has a plan for you life. He has a plan to prosper you and give you an expected end (Jeremiah 29:11). Following Esther's example by asking others, especially your pray partners, to help you may be necessary if you are struggling to see any good in your situation. The best way to see yourself is to look at your reflection through another agent. Many of you use a mirror throughout the day to check your appearance. Don't be afraid to ask your prayer partners to help you see yourself and the good you may be missing.

On the contrary, if you are in the midst of a positive season where it's easy to focus on the good, then continue to enrich your spiritual walk by being prayerful and committed. Since you pray throughout every day, maybe your prayers may be times of refreshing and worship. During these seasons, you may be able to focus more on praying for others. Regardless of where you are, know that challenges will come. We have God's assurance that we will make it through.

What happens when you are challenged with a difficult situation? You tap into your supernatural power when you pray because God will be working in you to complete his work in you. Prayer changes situations as much as it changes the one praying. Your attitude arsenal will become more Christ-like as you continue to spend time with God.

Your attitude arsenal has four main characteristics that function as your weapons against negativity when faced with difficult situations: *courage, determination, hope,* and *faith.* All four work together when you pray, and all four must be maintained as you are prepared to face any situation. As you continue to pray, you learn what God's will is for you. Trust in God and trust that he will help you know what his will is in every situation.

Chapter 28

Courage

You have certain rights and privileges because you are a child of the Most High God. However, you have to be courageous and strong in order to withstand the opposition that the enemy throws your way in order to prevent you from receiving God's promises. The same admonishment God gave Joshua is also extended to our generation as we are also in a covenant relationship with the Father.

"Be strong and of a good courage: for unto this people shall thou divide an inheritance the land, which I swear unto their fathers to give them. Only be thou strong and very courageous, that thou may observe to do according to all the law, which Moses my servant commanded thee: turn not from it to the right hand or to the left, that thou mayest prosper whithersoever thou goest…. Have not I commanded thee? Be strong (confident) and of a good courage" (Joshua 1:6–7, 9, AMP).

We should draw our courage from confidence in God and his ability. As you continue to grow in your knowledge of God, you should become more confident and courageous in your walk with God. You can only declare over your life what you know to declare. The truth you know is what sets you free. That is why it is so important for you to regularly attend church. The enemy wants to pull you away from church so you will not hear the Word of God. You need to be in an atmosphere where you can hear from God. Sometimes the enemy's attacks can become so fierce that you stop "dodging the darts." Every dart he throws hits you! You cannot pray at home and hear from God because your soul has been so battered all week long. Instead of suffering silently at home, you need to get to a place where God can minister to you through your elder. You have to be determined to go to church regularly and hear from God.

Chapter 29

Determination

Unfortunately, determination cannot be taught! Being determined is a decision you have to make—it's having a don't-quit attitude no matter what hurdles you encounter. You must supply your own dose of determination. Being in mental assent is not the same thing as determination. Mental assent is simply agreeing with the Word of God. Just agreeing with the Word will not free you. Your determination is active. Determination requires you to make a decision to believe what God has said and throw off everything that hinders us and the sin that so easily entangles (Hebrews 12:1).

Because of her determination, Ruth said, "'Where you go I will go, and where you stay I will stay. Your people will be my people and your God my God. Where you die I will die, and there I will be buried. May the Lord deal with me, be it ever so severely, if even death separates you and me.' When Naomi realized Ruth was determined to go with her, she stopped urging her" (Ruth 1:16–18).

This same don't-quit attitude causes us to believe nothing can separate us from the love of Christ (Romans 8:35–39). We are focused on our goal and continue to strive toward achieving it. Determined people actively work toward the goal. When you are determined to achieve your goal, you do not need to be reminded every step of the way by something on the outside. Your attitude drives your actions and come from the inner self. You must trust the Holy Spirit to strengthen you and help you stay determined.

One of my favorite poems illustrates a determined attitude. I memorized it in junior high school and often look back over it to remind myself of the "don't-quit" attitude. Here is an excerpt:

"Don't Quit"

When things go wrong, as they sometimes will,
When the road you're trudging seems all uphill,
When the funds are low and the debts are high,
And you want to smile, but you have to sigh,
When care is pressing you down a bit,
Rest, if you must, but don't you quit.
Often the goal is nearer than
It seems to a faint and faltering man,
Often the struggler has given up
When he might have captured the victor's cup.
And he learned too late when the night slipped down,
How close he was to the golden crown.
So stick to the fight when you're hardest hit—
It's when things seem worst that you must not quit.

—Author unknown

Chapter 30

Hope

Before we discuss faith, we must look at hope. Abraham believed what God said regardless of how the situation looked. Which do you believe? Do you believe the Word of God is the truth in your life, or are you led and controlled by how the situation looks in the natural? Hope initiates your faith. You must have hope before you can have faith. Hoping in the natural means you are dependent upon situations and circumstances to stay the same.

Abraham did not believe in natural hope. Abraham believed in spiritual hope (he believed God's Word rather than the situation). Spiritual hope is expecting something good is about to happen. Abraham believed things were getting better and used spiritual hope to initiate his faith.

"Who against (natural) hope believed in (spiritual) hope, that he might become the father of many nations, according to that which was spoken, so shall thy seed be…. He staggered not at the promise of God through unbelief; but was strong in faith, giving glory to God" (Romans 4:18, 20, KJV; emphasis added).

Chapter 31

Faith

Hope initiates your faith. In order to exercise your faith, you must have spiritual hope first. There must be a switch from "the Word might be true in my life," to "the Word *is* true in my life." You cannot even stand in faith if you are using natural hope. Natural hope relies on temporal circumstances. You cannot stand in faith for something if you will be led by how things look in the natural. Natural hope relies on the premise that anything could happen. Your faith will be weak if it is based on natural hope. You must use your faith in order to *stop* the enemy. A product of using your faith is further root development and more fruit. The more your roots develop the more established you will become. You will have a right to operate in God's truth and expect manifestations of his Word in your life. You must be fervent and strong in your faith. If opposition comes against you, you must declare your rights as given to you by God's Word.

Your faith can limit God in what he can do in your life. We serve a limitless God, but we have seen examples in the Word where God's power is limited in what it can do because of a lack of faith. Mark describes what happens when Jesus returned to his hometown and was unable to perform any miracles (Mark 6:5–6). Jesus was only able to heal a few sick people because of their lack of faith. Was Jesus suddenly unable to perform miracles? No, rather the people lacked faith, and faith activates the power of God in your life.

How can you increase your faith? Faith depends on revelation. As you encounter each step outlined here, you will likely begin to increase your faith in that particular area as you really dig deep into the Word. God's plan for your life will be revealed at a greater extent. The greatest motivator to pray will come as you begin to see the fruit grow in your life by praying.

Faith is actively applying the Word of God in a particular situation. Resist the enemy by being steadfast in the faith. Abraham was the best example of standing in faith. He is the "father" of standing in faith. "Therefore it is of faith, that it might be by grace; to the end the promise might be sure to all the seed; not to that also which is of the faith of Abraham; who is the father of us all, (As it is written, I have made thee a father of many nations,) before him whom he believed, even God, who quickeneth the dead and calleth those things which be not as though they were" (Romans 4:16–17).

Let's pray for wisdom on how to use spiritual hope to initiate our faith.

Prayer of Faith

"And the peace of God, which transcends all understanding, will guard your hearts and your minds in Christ Jesus. Finally, brothers, whatever is true, whatever is noble, whatever is right, whatever is pure, whatever is lovely, whatever is admirable—if anything is excellent or praiseworthy—think about such things" (Philippians 4:7–8).

Father, thank you for your peace that guards my heart and my mind. I bind evil thoughts and think pure, lovely, and admirable thoughts. When the enemy tries to convince me of something, I will immediately open my mouth and declare what your Word says about that situation. I will not allow these thoughts to roam my mind unchecked. I realize the battleground is in my mind, and I use my sword and shield of faith to fight the good fight. Thank you for your Holy Spirit who makes intercession for me. Thank you for your comfort, amen.

Right now, make a decision to write any progress down in a prayer journal. Encourage yourself along the way. God is a God of order. Some things happen instantly. Thank God for those, but sometimes we have to wait. What should you be doing along the way? You should be expecting your answer or deliverance. Wake up every morning expecting to write something down. Maybe it's a change in your thought pattern about the situation. Perhaps you notice changes in your relationship with your spouse.

One of the biggest motivators to continue to pray is answered prayer. Start today keeping a prayer journal. When you start to see signs of answered prayer, record it. No matter how insignificant it may seem when compared to the situation, acknowledge the hand of God working in your life and begin to give him praise for what's happening.

Chapter 32

The Seven Steps

Step 1

Identify the situation. Do you know where to start? List three things in your prayer journal that you need to pray about right now. You may select things that worry you, or situations that have you frustrated. Perhaps you have circumstances that seem too dire for a happy ending. Decide which one is the priority right now and circle it. How do you decide which one to choose when you have so much need in your life? Start off slowly. Some situations require a deeper understanding of the Word and a more developed relationship with God. Do not worry that you will not get it right. God is able to do exceedingly more than whatever you could imagine according to his power that is at work within you (Ephesians 3:20).

We can see this more clearly in the amplified bible translation: "Now to him who, by (in consequence of) the action of his power that is at work within us, is able to carry out his purpose and do superabundantly, far over and above all that we dare ask or think infinitely beyond our highest prayers, desires, thoughts, hopes, or dreams" (Ephesians 3:20, AMP).

Start with one problem area in your life that you want to be the focus of your work here and let's begin. Do not be too broad. Focus specifically on what you are worried. Are you facing challenges with your children? Are you struggling in your relationship with your husband or wife? Well, let's focus on the root of the fear. Being specific means identifying the area in your children's lives where you are being challenged. Is one of your children being attacked in his or her health? Are you afraid your wife does not value or need you? Do you fear being alone forever if you are unmarried? Try completing this statement to help you be specific:

I am worried about _____

_____.

I fear that if it happens, I will _____

_____.

Step 2

Make a summary. Think about three or four words or short phrases that could be used to summarize that situation. What word best captures what you need to pray about (e.g., marriage; husband/wife; divorce; alone; relationships)? Write the words that apply to your situation in your journal.

Step 3

Determine the Scripture. Using your concordance, look up all the words you listed in step two and write down the Scripture containing each word. Most Bibles contain a concordance, or if you like, you can use a search engine to find one online. Some Smartphones even have concordance apps. Decide what works best for you. If you do not carry a Bible with you, you may want to consider using search engines or Smartphone apps. We have more access to the Word now more than ever before. Look up each of the words in the concordance and write down the Scriptures that are referenced. You will have to read each one in context to decide if it is appropriate. Spend time doing this step as these will be the Scriptures you will spend time praying. Go through them and ask for a discerning spirit to determine which apply to your situation. You will use the Scriptures in your prayers so you want to be sure that they apply.

How will you know if they apply? It's best to read which verses or chapters come before and after it. This may also be a good time to purchase a study Bible. Study Bibles are an excellent reference and are well worth your purchase as you take a more active approach to praying about situations. If you are unable to purchase one now, you need to make saving for one a priority.

Your journal should be set up like this:

Situation   Scripture
1.
2.
3.

Check Yourself

When you have found your Scriptures, you must think of anything you may be doing that sabotages this truth. Be reflective and honest. Continuing to engage in negative behavior will negate the good work that is being accomplished in that situation through the Holy Spirit. Moreover, neglecting to do what is right will sabotage your efforts. Do you tithe regularly? Are you praying for your neighbors?

As you begin reading the Word concerning your situation, you will find many of these Scriptures are promises God has given you. These promises are not free. Jesus was the ultimate sacrifice that allows us access to what God has promised, but many of the promises do require that you be in a position to receive them. Review what we discussed in the seven tips for establishing an effective personal prayer life, especially tip two. Make sure you do not have attitudes or are not displaying actions that would make you ineligible. Consider what God instructs us about humbling ourselves, praying, and seeking his face (2 Chronicles 7:14). He says that if we do this, he will hear us and heal our land.

Step 4
Speak It, Speak It, Speak It!

Say it out loud. Hear yourself say it. Think about what you are saying. Repeat it a few times. Remember our exercise earlier about the power of speaking. It may feel weird and you may wrestle with it. Ask the Holy Spirit to help you where you may be struggling with doubt. Mark writes about a father who asks for help overcoming his unbelief (Mark 9:24). You are going to have to make a decision to believe God no matter what you are facing, but the Holy Spirit is here to help you, and you should ask for his help all the time. You must remind yourself of the Greater One living within you, and you must declare the Word of God over your situation. As soon as the Word of God is challenged in your life, open your mouth and declare that what God's Word says is true in your life. Be immovable!

Step 5
Show Gratitude

Having an attitude of thanksgiving and praise allows you to have a more God-centered prayer. Sometimes we face challenges that require us to hasten to the throne of grace and we rush right into what we need. This should be the exception and not the practice. We want to show gratitude instead of always having a needs-centered prayer. During this time, you should express to God how much you appreciate him and love him. Sometimes you may cite specific instances in your life that you are thanking him for, or you may use your own words to talk with him about how awesome he is.

Step 6
Strengthen Your Mind

How do you strengthen your mind? You strengthen your mind by renewing it. Renewal means reestablishing your thoughts, actions, and desires with the Word of God. A renewed mind is a strong mind. It is a mind that is able to discern God's will and apply it in certain situations. Because renewing your mind is a process, your mind may be renewed in one area and not another. Thus the complete renewal of your mind does not happen over night. It requires purposeful determination and effort. In order to renew your mind, you have to meditate on the Word. Meditate day and night. The tree that the psalmist describes is established and fruitful. Most fruit-bearing trees require time—sometimes years—before they begin to produce fruit. This metaphor found in the book of Psalms is preceded by the definition of the blessed man and what he does not do (sit stand walk) and what he does do. You all want to be that tree that's fruitful and prosperous but you must be willing to make the commitment to apply yourself to studying and reflecting on the Word- day and night.

So where do you start? Start with whatever topic you are praying about now. Start meditating on God's Word as it applies to this situation. Use your creative imagination to reflect and contemplate on what the Word would look like if it were manifested in your situation. Be faithful and read your Scripture cards every day, and you will begin to see fruit. It may not be a full harvest overnight, but do not become weary or frustrated when you are trying to do the right thing because you will reap your harvest if you do not give up (Galatians 6:9).

Scripture/prayer cards can be invaluable in establishing a healthy prayer life. You can make prayer stems from the Scriptures to use when you start to pray. When you pray, it is best to pray in the morning and evening as your day permits—remember, pray continually! For example, you may spend the next seven days praying your Scriptures. When you do this, do not be afraid to substitute your name or place or situation into the Scripture. When you begin doing this faithfully, surround yourself with believers who are hearers and doers of the Word. Use your prayer partners! These are people who find pleasure in the things of God, who also value his Word in their life. These people will support your efforts and help you carry the burden. Is there a relationship you have that is detrimental or someone who scorns your efforts? Surround yourself with the prayers from your prayer partners. Do not listen to well-meaning friends who keep telling you his or her opinion of what you should do in that situation.

Stand secure and continue to pray. When you hear news about it or something happens, continue to stand in prayer about it. Do not limit your prayers to just you and what you are facing. You have two legs. One leg represents the prayers for you. The other leg represents the prayers you have for others. You do not want to be lopsided. Pray for others who may also be experiencing the same challenge. If you know someone be specific if not pray use your daily prayers found in chapter three to continue praying for others.

Step 7
See It

When will you see complete manifestation of the promise in your life? Focus on the promise keeper, not just the promise. Your purpose should always be that God's plan be done in and through your life. The ultimate goal in each step should be for God to be glorified in your situation. Humble yourself and be willing to accept that how the promise looks when it is manifested in your life may or may not be exactly as you imagined it. When this is your focus, you will be able to face without uncertainty or fear what God has willed. God is a good God and ultimately you will have complete victory in every area of your life, either in this life or the next. Because you are a believer, you know this life is not the end.

"All these people were still living by faith when they died. They did not receive the things promised; they only saw them and welcomed them from a distance. And they admitted that they were aliens and strangers on earth. People who say such things show that they are looking for a country of their own. If they had been thinking of the country they had left, they would have had opportunity to return. Instead, they were longing for a better country—a heavenly one. Therefore God is not ashamed to be called their God, for he has prepared a city for them" (Hebrews 11:13–16).

Jesus has gone to prepare a world for us, and in this place we will be neither worried nor concerned with anything that does not line up with the Word of God (John 14:1–4). Wondering when you will see means you are expecting to see that promised fulfilled in your life, but it also means you recognize that the ultimate promise God has given is that you will be with him for an eternity. God will never leave you, but you must be willing to invest in your relationship with him. So why pray? God wants us to look for him in our situation. Looking for God's promises for you and your situation as outlined here means you are seeking him and his righteousness. If you are not looking for him and what he said about your situation, then you aren't seeking him. Remember, we want the promise maker, not just the promise!

Seven Steps toward Unleashing Supernatural Strength in Difficult Situations

The Fifth Scroll

Your attitude arsenal has four main characteristics that function as your weapons against negativity when faced with difficult situations: *courage, determination, hope and faith.*

God is able to do exceedingly more than whatever you could imagine according to his power that is at work within you (Ephesians 3:20).

Go through the scriptures and ask for a discerning spirit to determine which apply to your situation.

Make sure that you have do not have attitudes or that you are not displaying actions that would make you ineligible.

Renewal means reestablishing your thoughts, actions, and desires with the word of God.

Wondering when you will see means you are expecting to see that promised fulfilled in your life but it also means that you recognize that the ultimate promise that God has given is that you will be with him for an eternity.

Conclusion

The Word of God provides all the secrets for defeating every super villain in your life. God has provided the answers in his Word, but sometimes we have to seek them out. God knows the villains' weaknesses. Without that knowledge, we will get beaten up every time.

Pick up the Bible and find all the Scriptures that address your circumstance, and let's get started on our journey. Will you get discouraged when the enemy sends in his super villains? We are the original superheroes, and unlike the superhero in the cartoon I mentioned at the beginning of the book, we know it's our "holy DNA" that gives us the victory. We must be willing to pray—it is our ultimate weapon.

American evangelist, pastor, educator, and writer Reuben A. Torrey (1856–1928) wrote, "Those persons who know the deep peace of God, the unfathomable peace that passeth all understanding, are always men and women of much prayer."

You must be willing to tap into the supernatural power that lives on the inside of all believers in order to experience, accomplish, and possess all that God has for you. You are the *real* superhero!

About the Author

Lischa T. Brooks is a freelance writer who has served as an award-winning educator for more than sixteen years in the Memphis public school system. As a graduate of Dartmouth College, Lischa was a Mellon Fellow and received praise for creative writing. Currently, she works as a Professional Development Coordinator and has presented at the local and national level. She is married to H. Brandon Brooks, and they serve faithfully at the Life Church of Memphis, which is one of the fastest growing churches in the country. Together with their two children and goddaughter, they live in Cordova, TN. In her spare time, Lischa enjoys traveling, reading, and praying.